I Feel Your Stare

An Autobiography

•

Cheryl Gillespie

I Feel Your Stare

© Cheryl Gillespie 2022

First Paperback Edition ISBN 978-0-9950056-6-2

Follow the author on Facebook: www.facebook.com/Thebraillenarrative/[1]

Editing, typesetting and layout by Lee Thompson Editing+ Cover image, Adobe Stock.

This is a book of nonfiction. Some names and identifying details

of some individuals have been changed. Credits:

Photograph of Grand Falls, Chapter 3, Suzanne Légère.

Chapter 10. Nova Scotia Archives: School for the Blind, University Avenue, Halifax, N.S., Notman Studio, photographer; NSA, Notman Studio Collection, 1983-310 no. For Table of Contents 6999 (scan 200715108).

Other photos by Shelia and Joan Gillespie.

All rights reserved. No part of this publication may be reproduced or transmitted in any form or by any means, electronic or mechanical, including photocopying, recording, or any information storage and retrieval system, without permission in writing from the publisher.

---

1. http://www.facebook.com/Thebraillenarrative/

I Feel Your Stare
An Autobiography

•

Cheryl Gillespie

I Feel Your Stare, eloquently written by Cheryl Gillespie, is an intimate view of a truly remarkable life. In this autobiography, Cheryl leads us through an implausible childhood diagnosis of a chronic disease, which sets forth an ominous journey of gradual sight loss leading to total blindness.

Cheryl recounts her vivid memories of each formidable hurdle, and how she and her family tackled every setback with courage, strength, dignity and tenacity. The roller coaster of emotions I experienced while immersed in this book ranged from the most exquisite of highs, to waves of heartache – from wanting to jump up and high-five a superb demonstration of intellectual showmanship, to falling into an abyss of self exploration in asking myself 'how would I have handled that?'

You will fall in love with so many members of Cheryl's family and inner circle. You will laugh, you will cry, you will be thinking about this book long after you've turned the last page.

~Mary McGinley

I Feel Your Stare is a narrative of life experiences which take you into [Cheryl's] world, fostering an appreciation of those around us who may be viewed as different or less able but are in fact, as capable as anyone else. In her autobiography, we are challenged to think about how our society separates us rather than building a community, one which supports diversity and inclusion.... I would recommend this book to those of all ages who enjoy non-fiction, and the realities that shape the people around us, lending to an understanding that there is more to someone than what we see on the outside.

~Elizabeth Morrison

I Feel Your Stare reads as a powerful story of Cheryl Gillespie's courage. In early childhood the author is forced to live with the pain of Juvenile Rheumatoid Arthritis and associated blindness, and yet, is able to find joy, purpose and humour in her life. Strength is evident in her stubborn independence, in a supportive husband and family, her music and in her Christian faith.

As physicians we often learn from our patients, and to this end, Cheryl Gillespie has been a great teacher. Thank you for the lesson that when we do not have good answers to relieve suffering there is a decisive value in listening.

~Stephen Hart M.D.

Chapters

The Braille Mirror
Early Life in Morrell Siding: Mother's Journal
The Diagnosis (1960s)
The Guardian Angel
An Endless Horrible Dream
Starting School
A Heartrending Decision (1970s)
Summer Vacation
World's Apart
Eye of The Storm
Good 'Riddins' to Goodbyes
Culture Shock
Black and Gold (1980s)
Me and Old Willis
Imperfect Harmony
My Cares, My Prayers
In Good Times, And in Bad (2000s)
Song of Luminescence
Acknowledgements
About the Author

Chapter 1
THE BRAILLE MIRROR

January: the month of fresh renewal for the future, and yet, tunes of old memories play in my head over and over again. On this winter's night, my fingers caress the piano keys of a soul-searching melody. Wishing it to last, I prolong the final chord until it fades to silence.

Spoiling the moment, a bluster of flurries pelts against the window screen. The wind; Michael hated that. It spooked him, and like a prowling tiger he'd pace back and forth across the floor of our little bungalow. Curious how a gust of wind reminds me of Michael. Then again, so many things do, especially since his passing.

On a nearby table awaits a piping cup of hot cocoa. As tightly as I dare, I coddle it until my palms feel a warm tingling sensation, then set it down again.

The snow squall subsides, and once more a hush falls over the coziness of my piano room. Ahh! Solitude! This is a welcome friend, as it's when I'm the most creative. On the other hand, loneliness is an unwanted foe, always lurking around the next corner.

Those dreadful goodbyes — I've come to the realization of how much this has imprinted on who I am today. As I trace the experiences from my youth, it defines why I am hesitant to get close to others, or why it is difficult to show my true feelings.

For me, music has always been my sanctuary, an intangible but soft place to land. Michael and I had this in common, an unmistakeable bond shared between us.

Essential as it is to me in the present, music is a constant link to my past. A particular tune is heard on the radio, and in an instant I am doodling with Spirograph at the Montreal Children's Hospital, or pouring over home- work in my dormitory at the Halifax School for the Blind. It's not all about those separations from my loved ones, though. Music has given me fond memories of singing in church, concert performances with Michael, and of course, my piano-teaching career, which has been near to my heart for more than three decades.

Whether in a song, a touch, or a smell, I often find myself transported to an episode which occurred long ago. Of course, I know it happens to everyone. Overall, these sensory trips take me somewhere happy, but there are times when it can be downright frightening!

•

As the snow accumulates outside, I recognize my own emotional barriers, the ones built between certain childhood incidents and the present day. Recently, these metaphoric walls have been assaulted, the harsh glare of present realities exposing what I had so carefully guarded.

During the worldwide COVID-19 pandemic, I kept a medical appointment, fully anticipating being screened with myriad questions. I did not, however, expect to be thrust into my childhood, simply by an order to wear a face- mask. It shouldn't have been a big deal, but it was. Scents of hospital disinfectants drifted into my nose, making me lightheaded. And if that weren't enough, I suppressed the panic as ghouls in scrubs who had once stared down at me began to invade my thoughts.

I imagine it's easy for those to judge, saying, "Aren't you being melodramatic?" Honestly, I thought I was over it. I was five years old when *that* surgeon gave me his word, but he lied! He had promised not to use a mask over my face, the one which pumped out that noxious sleeping gas. Evidently, there were no intentions on his part to administer an injection, as I had pleaded. The struggle that ensued between us on the operating table was unforgivable! How could he do that to a child?

•

Back at home, visions of the past chased me straight into my bathroom. Grabbing a facecloth, I used an excessive amount of soap and water to cleanse my face again and again. The odour refused to go away. Now what? I needed mouthwash to eliminate that obscene operating-room taste. "Stop it," I cried, and from that time onward, if a mask were required during the public health crisis, I vowed to wear a scarf, a garment which would not stimulate disturbing childhood flashbacks.

•

In contrast, pleasant aromas will carry me elsewhere, to childhood destinations in which I contentedly linger. Homemade bread? Well, that takes me to my grandmother Gillespie's farm kitchen, where she was up baking at the crack of dawn. Pickles and herbs? That was my grandmother Goodine's house. There, one could almost taste the fruits of her labour — the scent of mingled flavours from her garden was the first thing to greet you at the door.

•

I reach for my hot cocoa, take another sip. Mmm! That conjures up more memories. Whenever we kids stayed at Grandma Goodine's, this, along with a topping of cinnamon and sugar on toast, was always a favourite bedtime treat for us.

Indeed, my mother was a Goodine. What on earth would I have done without her throughout the years?

She, after all, was the one who has played the most profound role in my life.

Upon reflection of my story, I'm compelled to connect the dots of my mother's youth, since it relates to my own journey into the present. It's uncanny, as though we've had somewhat parallel lives. I can only speculate, but I have to wonder if she were perhaps immunocompromised if only for a brief time? Is it not peculiar that she endured arthritic pain in her teens, or those bizarre incidents as a child when her eyesight was at risk? What's more, is the significance of her name a fluke, or was it all a part of God's plan?

Toward that end, throughout this narrative I opt to express her thoughts in a journal, suitably called, *Cecilia*. As I unfold relative backstory, I'll begin with my mother and the setting of her family homestead, in the scenic countryside of northwest New Brunswick.

Chapter 2
EARLY LIFE IN MORRELL SIDING:
Mother's Journal

Through her upstairs bedroom window, a dismal view of overcast skies, and the April snow a dirty brown from the spring thaw. An ominous chill hovered in the west where, tragically, a B-52 bomber from Loring Air Force Base in Maine had crashed into a snow-packed hillside, leaving only one survivor. This had been a terrible shock for their rural community, and years later, people were still able to comb the dense forest to find scattered debris from the wreckage. "I wonder what Grandma would have thought of all of this?" she pondered.

Although it didn't seem that long ago, it was seven years since the sad passing of her beloved grandmother. When at last their family had moved into the Goodine homestead, the elderly woman was known to say, "I'm so happy you are all living here! Besides, there's plenty of room, and it's high time someone looked after me."

Stepping away from the window, she turned to the inviting allure of her room. There, spread over her bed, was Mama's homemade quilt, a soft lavender embroidered with tiny white flowers. At the foot of the bed, a hope chest where she'd sit to face a wooden table, upon which lay her schoolbooks, paper and pencils. With her Grade 12 English assignment finished, she opened her personal journal, and began to peruse its various entries.

•

Dear Cecilia:

If it's all the same to you, perhaps, I might consider you as a distant twin. After all, my name, Shelia, is derived from the Latin for Cecilia. I only wish Cecilia didn't mean 'blind.' How strange! And yet, I suppose I have had a few incidents of my own when my vision was jeopardized.

On a positive note, St. Cecilia, born in second or third century Rome, was the patron saint of music. Oh, I much prefer this side of your identity! Not that I'm a musician myself, but I love listening to the waltzes or lively jigs and reels Father plays on fiddle, sometimes accompanied by Mama on a dance-hall piano. So, my dear Cecilia, it's as though your name were a mysterious, puzzle piece of my life.

On the other hand, I'm comforted to know that my surname, Goodine, originates from the name Godin, meaning 'God' or 'good.' The Goodine lineage traces back to France, from where they migrated to Quebec, and eventually settled in New Brunswick. The house where we now live was built by my great grandfather, the last French-speaking generation of the Goodine family.

I could write a ton of memories of this old house: like the times when downstairs, Grandma used to sit on the glassed-in porch where year-round geraniums of red, white and purple bloomed in each window. There, Grandma would listen to my endless chatter of school classmates, the upcoming church picnic, or a bit of juicy neighbourhood gossip.

I have earlier memories, too. Before we moved to Grandma's, I recall living in a modest cedar house — the one where I was born. From its backyard I could glance upward and see, on the horizon, the rolling hills of the Appalachian Mountain range. Eastward lay a small farm built on a hillside, just across the long, flowing river. By day, a farmer could be seen cutting hay and at evening the family dog rounded up the cows to bring them in for milking. To the west, another hillside, this one cleared for pasture with an untouched forest crowning its lofty peak.

As a child, I remember skipping down the gravel road to my grandparent's homestead where Grandma ran a small country store. "Grandma!" I'd squeal. "Mama would like to buy a dozen eggs, please." While she gathered the small purchase, I'd gaze around the foyer lined with shelves stocked with an odd assortment of items, like tea, peanut butter, thread, safety pins and chicken feed.

"Here you are, darling," Grandma would say, while passing me a basket of freshly-laid eggs from the chickens she raised. "Oh, and here is a little treat for you." I knew if I stared at the small candies in the store long enough, Grandma would give me a toffee "BB Bat" to eat on the way home.

Careful not to drop the basket, I'd walk along the roadside breathing in the country air, fragrant with newly mown hay, fresh rain and clover. By dusk, though, we were sure to get a strong whiff of smoke from the smudges intended to keep the blackflies away.

At our brown cedar house, a simmering pot of beef stew was on the wood stove along with fresh vegetables from Mama's garden, and on the countertop, a basin of water carried from the backyard brook for washing. During hot summer days, we bathed in that little spring-fed brook cascading down the sloped hillside. At night, I'd listen to its familiar trickle through my open window and soon be lulled into a sound sleep.

In the morning, after a filling bowl of porridge, I'd run outside to freshen up, and there — the hillside where I once climbed to pick a bouquet of wild flowers for Mama. I'll never forget the moment I accidentally stepped in a hornets' nest, lost my balance and rolled down the hill. Hearing my loud cries, Mama hurried to my rescue as the hornets had stung me countless times.

Within a few days of applying baking soda and water, my stings had remarkably healed.

After breakfast, we were off berry picking. Mama would carry a one-gallon lard pail, empty after a winter of baking. When she announced, "Here's a good spot," we'd each take a metal cup used to dip in the brook for drinking, fill it with berries, and dump them into Mama's huge pail.

Around noontime, we would stretch a blanket over a grassy mound, rest, and have something to eat. For lunch, Mama brought sliced homemade bread, already buttered, and milk in small pickle jars to drink. With a fork she'd mash the berries, nicely warmed by the sun, lightly sprinkle them with sugar, and spread them over the bread — so delicious!

"Like all kids, I'd always sport a healthy bronze tan and sprout up about an inch taller under the summer sunshine. I do recall, however, when our doctor decided that I was too thin, and recommended that Mama feed me eggnog to fatten me up, as well as a daily spoonful of cod liver oil to improve my immune system. I liked Mama's eggnog, made of raw egg and unpasteurized milk, sweetened with maple flavouring. The awful tasting cod liver oil was another matter. Yuck! I hated seeing that dreaded brown bottle, depicting a man who proudly held up a cod fish.

As for my winter memories — with no streetlights on our country road, it was the moon and stars which lit the night sky. Looking up, I easily spotted the big and little dipper, and looking down, I'd see my shadow cast on the frosty snow.

With unsettled weather, Mama would check the thermometer outside the kitchen window then peer down the road at the neighbour's chimney. If the smoke was going straight up, she knew there was no wind. After all, the little school, two miles away from our house, made for a very cold walk during winter months. On occasion, our teacher's husband might give us a ride but not often, as it was a lot of work to harness the horses and hitch up the sleigh.

Following those heavy snowstorms, we were often kept from walking to school as the roads would not be plowed for three or four days. This was a fun time for all of us — my siblings, my cousins and I — to go sliding on a long toboggan with room enough for five or six kids. "You can sit in the front seat," my sister Joyce and cousin Fred persuaded me, since I was the youngest in the group. Little did I know, the person at the front was the one to get their face washed with a spray of fresh snow.

•

All at once, her reading was interrupted by a faraway whistle of the 10-a.m. train, signalling its departure from the station. It reminded her of when she and Grandma would rush to the front stoop and wave to her father, who was the conductor. Feeling its rumble past the home of her aunt, uncle and nine cousins, they'd watch until the train would disappear — well beyond the shade of the apple trees.

She released her fingers from the diary and positioned her hands behind her back, adding pressure to massage her spine. Occasionally it bothered her, arthritis having set in after an incident three years earlier when she had fallen on the ice and injured her tailbone.

"That's better," she sighed, resting her arms on the wooden table.

Just then, there came a knock at the downstairs front door leading to the large foyer where Grandma once kept her little store. "Who could that be?"

"Thank you, and have a nice day," she overheard Mama's words as money was handed to the local fish peddler.

"Oh, that's who it was," she muttered. Tugging a pillow from her bed, she propped it behind her and leaned into it for support. She then thumbed to the next page of her journal and continued to browse through the excerpts.

•

Dear Cecilia:

A lot has changed since our family moved to Grandma's house. For instance, electricity has come to the community, so no longer are the old wood stove, kerosene lamps, or the scrub board and tub used for doing laundry.

What's more is the absence of my older sisters, Joyce and Alberta. They have long since left home, received their nursing diplomas, and are now married.

I too, have met someone. Martin is handsome, tall and slender. His family's farm is in Gillespie Settlement, about fifteen miles away. I expect he'll be job hunting soon, as Martin has already completed his trade school course, receiving a certificate in Mechanical Drafting.

By now, everyone must know about Martin and I going steady, given that our crank telephone is on a party-line with other families in the valley. You see... it's no secret that old Mrs. Dexter is notorious for eavesdropping on private conversations, as revealed by the chipper singing of her pet canary in the background. Oh, silly woman! If only she could snoop in my diary, she would discover that Martin and I have been recently engaged.

•

Before she knew it, the countryside was alive again as summer brought the sweet smell of timothy hay, vibrant colours to fields and gardens, birds nesting, and a new colt born at her uncle's farm across the gravel road. With high school graduation behind her, she and Mama busied themselves making all the arrangements for her upcoming marriage to Martin Gillespie.

When the day arrived, she gazed into her bedroom mirror, carefully adding a few curls to her straight, honey-brown hair. She was pleased with the wedding dress which her mother had made: a royal blue, practical to wear for future occasions. Just then, the eighteen-year-old spotted the journal on her dresser, the one penned with youthful sentiments. She realized how much she would miss this house and the simple life she had growing up in Morrell Siding. Gently, she lifted the journal and tucked it between the layers of clothing within her hope chest. She was certain there would be something to write in it tomorrow, and all her tomorrows after that. At last, flipping back the wispy curls from her shoulders, she smoothed out her beautiful dress and opened the bedroom door, calling out, "Mama! I'm ready!"

Chapter 3
THE DIAGNOSIS

As newlyweds, my parents, Shelia and Martin began their life together at the homestead in Gillespie Settlement. Although I have few details of this period, I am certain that the heart of the home was the kitchen. I'm told that there were ten people living under one roof, and to make for a larger crowd, farmhands often joined the family for early breakfasts, a big spread at noontime, and for leftovers in the evening.

While living in the settlement, Dad worked for his older brother, Marshall, who ran the family farm. He looked up to Marshall, a hardworking man, and one who brought laughter to all who knew him.

I have no doubt that my parents look back on these times from a different perspective, but I tend to imagine it with a quaint nostalgia based solely on the childhood memories I had when visiting my grandparents. There's just something about that big old house, the sustenance of the land, the decency of the people which captures that enduring connection to the past.

Not long ago, I had the opportunity to visit the Gillespie estate, presently in the care of my cousin, Anne. In one of the five upstairs bedrooms was a trunk filled with family treasures. My attention was drawn to a letter of reference written by the local mayor, a charmingly styled script conveying my father to be a worthy candidate in his search for employment.

To Whom It May Concern,

Mr. Martin G. Gillespie, of Grand Falls, NB, is a young man of good character and reputation, being a descendant of old pioneer families of this community. I am pleased to recommend him for his dependability and trustworthiness, commending him to your most favourable consideration.

Yours respectfully,

M.F. McCluskey, Mayor

After six months on the farm, Mom and Dad moved to the nearby town of Grand Falls, my father having secured a position with the New Brunswick Power Commission. Perfect timing, as my mother was expecting me, their first baby.

I like to think I arrived into the world wearing a pink bow on my head! Oh well...what I can say for sure, is that I was born during our Canadian Thanksgiving, a season where the October foliage paints the landscape in a vivid canvas of red and gold.

Meanwhile, with vacation from NB Power coming to my father he felt it best to use this time to earn some extra money for his growing family, and work the harvest back at the farm. In his absence, my aunt Joyce stepped up and offered to stay by Mom's side at the hospital. Even so, Joyce did not expect colleagues to toss a gown in her direction, requesting her presence at the birth.

Afterward, my mother recounts her sister's words, "When I promised I'd be with you, I didn't mean I'd be in the delivery room!"

•

By age twenty-two, Mom's days were centred around her husband, her children and the house they had rented in Grand Falls. I was two years old, my brother Thomas was one, and her third baby was on the way. With all of this, she began to consider everything her own mother had done for them — the huge garden of vegetables and herbs that Mama planted, and the nights when she sat up late, knitting and sewing clothes or blankets. Along with raising a family of six, her mother fostered two more children, and it wasn't uncommon to see her taking a home-cooked meal to the sick or shut-in. "How was Mama able to do it all?" she pondered, especially where her father's work on the railroad often took him away from the family.

History has a peculiar way of repeating itself. Similar to my grandfather Goodine, Dad was also out of town for days or weeks at a time working as a linesman throughout the province. I too marvel at my mother's resilience and her resourcefulness. Mind you, she made it look easy. I remember instances like when buying groceries, she'd pick up the telephone, place an order and voila, the items were delivered to our home in several brown paper bags. Still, I'm in awe: not that everything associated with keeping a two-storey house and caring for kids wasn't a task in itself, but when a child is seriously ill, day to day life becomes far more intense.

And so it began. Standing in the living-room, Mom methodically ironed clothes, folded and arranged them into a neat pile on a chair. Just then, she noticed that I had toddled over and rested my little hand on the stack of clothes, newly warmed from the iron. Upon closer look, Mom saw that my wrist was swollen, and that I was protective of it. "No, Mummy, no!" I fussed, pulling my hand away and placing it back on the soothing warmth of the clothes.

This didn't seem right! She knew something was off with my behaviour, along with my inflamed wrist. Taking no chances, Mom immediately made an appointment for me with a doctor in Grand Falls.

•

"How could *you*, as the child's mother, not know how her wrist had been so badly sprained?" The doctor's tone was accusing. For one fleeting moment, she began to doubt herself as a mother. Her mind raced — have I neglected Cheryl, or done anything that might have hurt my baby girl? And now...this man is insinuating child abuse? How dare he! Regaining her composure, Mom indignantly shook her head. No, she concluded, this quack is out of line and has no idea what he is talking about!

Time passed, and my wrist worsened, which prompted a second visit to that scowling doctor. "You can't let her favour her wrist," he said gruffly. "You must bend it and make her use it, otherwise it will become deformed in growth." Showing no compassion, the man then took my swollen wrist and forcefully bent it. As though struck by a flaming arrow, the shriek of pain which came from me will forever be seared into my mother's heart.

"Stop it right now!" she ordered. As I cried uncontrollably, Mom gathered me up, saying, "Don't you ever touch my child again!"

It had been weeks since Mom first saw me rest my hand on that warm stack of clothes. After raising concerns to her sister, Mom learned about a doctor from Scotland who had recently established his practice in Perth. With one phone call, the new family physician agreed to see me on a Saturday, a convenient time for Dad to drive us to the neighbouring town.

•

In mid January, temperatures had plummeted into a deep freeze. From outside, a grinding noise could be heard as Dad attempted to start and warm up the old car, on loan to him from Marshall.

"It's no use!" he declared, brushing the snow from his boots. "The battery is dead. Should we postpone the appointment until next Saturday?"

Mom thought of her father-in-law, a kind man, and often a kidder. On very cold winter days he'd telephone to ask, "Did your car start today?" He liked to rub it in, especially after his recent purchase of an Oldsmobile, and jokingly bragged his car would start in 50 degrees below.

Feeling a nagging sense that they should not wait, Mom replied, "Please call your father and ask him if he will drive us to Perth."

•

When we arrived at the clinic, Dr. Thompson examined me and immediately knew what was wrong. "I have seen cases like this before when I lived in Scotland. I don't mean to scare you..." The doctor's words trailed into an empty silence, the urgency in his voice prompting alarm for my mother. "I'd like to admit Cheryl into hospital today and run tests for Juvenile Rheumatoid Arthritis."

Dr. Thompson's suspected diagnosis was confirmed. Test results for my white-blood-cell count were so off the charts that it was impossible to assess. Indeed, my immune system was attacking my own body, causing the inflammation; and by this time, it had spread to other joints.

This was devastating news for Mom, Dad, and our families. At a time when church doors were never locked, my Goodine and Gillespie grandparents would often be found inside — kneeling in prayer for their suddenly ill granddaughter.

•

At the Perth hospital, it was not permitted for guardians to visit their sick children — a policy closely observed to keep the youngsters from crying after their parents had left. For Mom, this separation was agonizing! Consequently, provided she did not let me spot her, the nurses allowed my mother to watch through a window covered with venetian blinds.

With unyielding glass between us, Mom could see that I was lying in my crib, eyes closed. For the first two weeks, Dr. Thompson was uncertain whether I would live or die. This was inconceivable! Mom shuddered, thinking that if they had postponed the appointment on that bitterly cold day, she could have lost her baby girl forever.

•

It was late February and with my father working out of town, Mom's parents offered to drive her to the hospital. Through the slats of the blinds, eyes fixed on me, she thought of the long conversations with her grandmother on the glassed-in porch of the Goodine homestead. She recalled the story of Grandma's own daughter, Ann, who died prematurely, before her third birthday. The child never learned to walk, likely due to joint pain. Dr. Thompson had related that cases of JRA are genetic, so it was highly probable that little Ann had the disease but at that time there were no methods for it to be diagnosed.

Gazing longingly through the venetian blinds, Mom noticed that I was alert and looking around. "There's my Mummy! There's my Mummy!" I called out, pointing to the window.

"You have to let her go in!" my grandmother Goodine demanded of the nurses. "Cheryl has seen her. You have to let her go in, now!"

Mom was immediately ushered into my hospital room. Trembling, she picked me up, holding back her tears. Following this incident, the hospital staff made an exception for Mom and from then onward, she was allowed to visit me anytime she wished.

My lengthy hospital stay was exhausting for her, particularly with baby three on the way. It was comforting news when Mom learned that the nurses had also granted visitation to grandparents and extended family members. How much she had come to appreciate my uncle Jack, Joyce's husband, who'd frequently visit me on his lunch break, sit me on his lap and rock me to sleep.

Hours stretched into days, and the days into weeks. To everyone who passed by my door, I watched and listened intently, asking, "Is that Mummy?" Clearly, I was lonely — and to make matters worse, mealtimes had become a struggle with "No, I don't like it!" while my little hands pushed the food away. As my health relapsed, concerned nurses began to take desperate measures. Staring into my jade-green eyes, nurse Ollie pinched my nose, forcing my mouth open so she could slip in a spoonful of mush. Unfortunately, all of this had become counter productive to my wellbeing. Instead of getting better, much of my energy was spent fighting battles, mistrusting of my caregivers and yearning to go home.

After three months, Dr. Thompson decided to discharge me from hospital — not that I had recovered but because I was homesick and wouldn't eat. He recommended

Mom and I stay at Aunt Joyce's house for a couple of weeks as he felt comfortable knowing she was a nurse and we would be closer to the hospital.

When Mom and I finally arrived at our home in Grand Falls, we began a regular routine of warm baths, physiotherapy exercises to strengthen my muscles and medications every four hours. All in all, this first arthritis flare-up had lasted nine months from start to finish.

Chapter 4
A GUARDIAN ANGEL

After months of daily exercise, my leg muscles became stronger and I was able to walk again. However, just like the awful cod-liver-oil episodes in my mother's own childhood, I objected to the pills that I was to take every four hours. My stubborn protests to be fed while in hospital were due to their futile attempt to disguise my medications within the food. Recognizing the predicament, Mom determined she would not betray my trust, but instead resolved the matter with a bit of tough love.

"Cheryl," she explained. "I won't hide the medicine in your food. I will either put it in your hand and you can take it yourself, or I will have to pinch your nose like nurse Ollie." Though only two years old, I understood my options. Mom wasn't fooling around! Cautiously, I reached out my hand and shoved the tablets in my mouth. Eww! A sour look came over my face as I chewed up the pills, and washed them down with a cold drink of water.

Sadly, this period of remission was short lived. When Mom came home from the hospital with baby number four, she knew right away by looking at me that the illness had returned. After a day of observing my movements and behaviour, she immediately telephoned Dr. Thompson. It was mid-December when, for the second time, I was hospitalized for juvenile rheumatoid arthritis.

On December 25th, Mom posed a brave face while visiting me in the Perth hospital. She looked down and there I lay asleep, wearing a pink and white nightgown. "How uncomfortable her little legs must be," she thought, observing that they were kept immobile by splints, wrapped with strips of cotton gauze. "This should be a magical day for a four-year-old girl..."

Sitting by my crib, she remembered an incident which had taken place the previous year. It was after midnight when Mom was awakened from a deep sleep, startled by my loud cries. Frantic, she rushed to the nearby bedroom, reached into the crib and picked me up. On that night, I had awakened to see a human-like silhouette, surrounded by light in the upstairs window. Between sobs and trying to catch my breath, I motioned toward the tasseled curtains and stammered, "Mummy! — A light! — The moon passed me by! — It looked at me!"

Mom had heard enough to be convinced that I had seen some kind of vision. She believed in her heart that guardian angels watched over small children, and if the child died, they would carry them away to Heaven. Upset by the night's event, Mom had called Joyce the following day and blurted into the phone, "They're going to take my baby!"

In this moment, a sick feeling came over her as she relived that frightful memory of nearly losing her first-born daughter.

Just then, I opened my eyes, delighted to see my mother on Christmas day. "Look Mummy! See what Santa brought?" I pointed to a long red stocking speckled with tiny snowflakes hanging at the foot of my crib. At the top of the stocking was a striped candy cane and inside there were two oranges and some small, wrapped gifts. When I awoke Christmas morning, I was met by another surprise sitting by my pillow. Anxious to show my mother, I cuddled *Star Bright,* a doll with black hair, wearing a pretty green velvet dress, with sparkling stars in her eyes. Caught up in my excitement, Mom told me, "When you come home, there are more presents that Santa left — just for you."

•

Six weeks passed before I could go home to my mother, father, and three younger siblings. Near the end of January, Dad carried me out of the brisk, wintery air, and into the warmth of our cozy house. Again, I was very frail and would face more home physiotherapy in the months ahead. Oh, how magical! Mom and Dad had left up a few Christmas decorations for my homecoming. I stared in amazement at the shimmering lights of red, yellow, green and blue, which twinkled against the silver garland. Perched on a corner shelf, an ornamental angel watched over our family, all of whom were gathered in the living-room. Beautiful, this angel did not frighten me, not like the one that had appeared in the upstairs bedroom window. Besides, I had to believe my mother's comforting words, "Don't worry. Guardian angels are there to keep us safe."

It was Christmas Day all over again. Happily, I played with a new little stove — just like Mummy's, along with some tiny cups and plates. In the corner of the room sat a toy piano, brownish-red, with eight tinkling keys. Listening carefully to each sound, I was able to pick out *Mary Had A Little Lamb,* and declared to my parents outright, "When I grow up, I'm going to play a real piano!"

Chapter 5
AN ENDLESS HORRIBLE DREAM

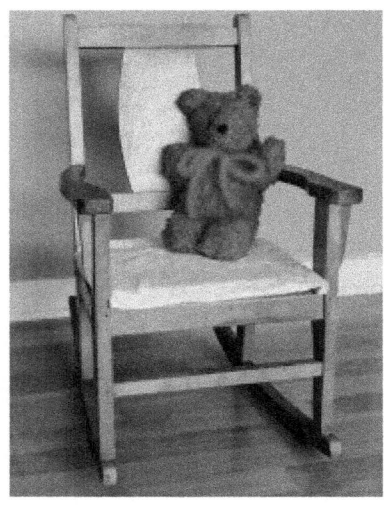

Raising four children while attending to a two-storey house, meant my mother's days would have to run like clockwork. For us kids, afternoon naps were from two until four, and bedtime was always at seven in the evening. When we slept, all was quiet, the perfect time for Mom to catch up on housework or perhaps grab an opportunity for a well-deserved rest.

In the early morning, Mom would gather Thomas, Susan, Joan and I around the table for breakfast, with "Captain Kangaroo" on TV in the background. After we had finished our cereal and orange juice, the day would be filled with fun activities: of tea parties, colouring, singing, games like, I Spy with My Little Eye, and outdoor skipping and hula-hoop.

A favourite time spent together, was when Mom read to us from a book of well-known fairy tales. Over and over again, we'd ask to hear the stories of *The*

Three Little Pigs, Jack and the Beanstalk, The Gingerbread Man, or *The Elves and the Shoemaker.*

In June, a few months after returning home from my most recent arthritis flare-up, Mom noticed that I couldn't see properly. As I tried to focus on TV, books, or objects across the room, she observed that I tilted my head to the right, to compensate for not seeing well from my left eye. "Time for another visit to the doctor," she decided, then picked up the phone and began to dial.

•

After a thorough eye exam, Dr. Thompson took a pen from his desk, pulled out the chart and jotted a few notes. "I was afraid of this," he spoke in a low voice. Looking up from his papers, he turned toward my mother. "I'm going to refer Cheryl to a top eye specialist at the Montreal Children's Hospital."

•

On a hot summer day, Dad loaded our suitcases into the trunk of his new, 1968 Pontiac Parisienne. "Best car I'll ever have," he boasted, slapping its misty green hood. All set to go, we started our journey to Quebec, a trip that would be taken many more times over the next five years.

Seven hours to Montreal seemed like an eternity, and during most of the drive, I'd be asleep in the back seat. When Dad stopped at a gas station, this was the time for treats — a bottle of orange pop and a bag of Hickory Sticks! It was an adventure when we came to the Louis La-fontaine Bridge Tunnel, which extended under the St. Lawrence River. It was fascinating to be in a dark passage with so many cars and overhead lights, and when we emerged on the other side, warm daylight appeared once again.

The big city of Montreal was much different than the town of Grand Falls. The streets were bumper-to-bumper traffic and the air was a fog of diesel exhaust — not like the fresh, clean air back in New Brunswick.

My first experience of eating in a restaurant was in Montreal. The waitress took the grown-ups' order, and then it was my turn. "I'd like a peanut butter and jam sandwich, please."

"Oh," Mom apologized, "I don't think they serve that here."

"It's no trouble," smiled the kind waitress. "I will make a peanut butter and jam sandwich for her. I don't mind at all."

•

When they met the distinguished Dr. John Little, an ophthalmologist and professor at McGill University, he informed my parents: "This condition is called uveitis — an inflammation of the eye tissues which affects children with JRA. Potentially, there can be more eye complications with this disease, but I assure you, Cheryl will receive the best care possible."

•

Lying in the hospital of a strange city, four hundred miles from my hometown, was no longer a pleasurable adventure. When surrounded by a throng of McGill University resident doctors, all of whom were studying my medical case, I wanted to run and hide. Prying my eyelids wide open, each intern held a harsh burning light and analytically peered into my eyes. Although I did not yet understand its meaning, overhearing Dr. Little utter the word "surgery" gave me a sense of uneasiness. The only thing I knew for certain was that I wanted to go home.

•

With my first eye operation behind me, I awakened and listened for my mother's familiar voice. Unable to change position, I squirmed uncomfortably. In order to keep me from sliding tiny fingers under the eye patch, my hands had been tied to the rails on either side of the bed. This disturbed my mother. "She isn't going to touch her eyes," Mom assured the nurses. "Cheryl has arthritis," she insisted, "and restricting her movement is causing her pain." Heeding my mother's wishes, a nurse reluctantly loosened the bands, and my hands were freed.

For several weeks I remained in hospital to undergo more observation, treatment and surgery. To my dismay, my parents could not stay in Montreal for such a lengthy time. Besides, Mom would never expect Aunt Joyce to keep my three siblings indefinitely, and soon, Dad would have to return to work.

"Will you go down to the gift shop and buy something that will keep her occupied while we're gone?" my mother urged. When Dad returned, he proudly presented Cocoa, a caramel-brown teddy bear with a big red bow. That wasn't quite what Mom had in mind, but as fate would have it, Cocoa became my trusted childhood companion.

During the weeks spent in Montreal, Cocoa and I were inseparable. "That doctor hurts me, so we won't talk to him, okay?" I whispered in his ear. "I like that nurse, though," I continued, pointing to a dark-haired woman, "because she gives me chocolate milk!"

Understanding that I was alone, nurse Maria took me under her wing. "You know," Maria said, "I am also a long way from my home."

"Oh, where do you live?"

"I'm from Spain, a country very far from here."

In the evening, Maria asked for my special assistance. "Would you like to deliver the nighttime snacks with me? I could sure use your help."

Pushing the cart from room to room, we offered each patient a variety of choices. "What would you like before bedtime?" There were beverages, melba toast, crackers and cheese, and even cookies and brownies.

•

On my return to Grand Falls, I encountered more physical and emotional trials. There were arthritis flare-ups, along with bi-weekly trips to the Perth hospital where I was put under general anaesthesia — this, in order to have cortisone injected into both eyes. It was unthinkable, but I was more afraid in the Perth hospital near my hometown than when I had faced surgery and endured painful tests in Montreal. Here, the method of inducing sleep was by using ether from a mask over the mouth and nose. Suffocating from its noxious odour, I heard a hissing; an unintelligible murmur of evil voices which echoed in my ears. Stricken with terror, I forcibly vanished into a place of darkness.

•

At the tender age of five, I was aware of more hospital procedures than most adults would ever realize. I begged the surgeon in Perth, "Please, will you use the needle to put me to sleep, like they do in Montreal?" The doctor promised me: he would do as I requested. Instead, when lying on the operating table, the mask was deliberately aimed at an angle where no unsuspecting child would ever see it. As the mask snuck up on me, I screamed and lashed out with my arms and legs in a struggle to get away. Merciless, the doctor over-powered me, and for decades to come, this experience would be severely traumatizing!

The result of this incident spawned a reoccurring nightmare. In my dream, I sat in the middle of a grassy plain. It was a faintly-lit night with crickets chirping. Sitting alone in this peaceful field, I heard a distant rhythmic thumping growing louder, and louder! As the sound neared, I could see a row of men marching toward me, wearing shields and carrying shiny swords. I was paralyzed with fear! Suddenly, I awoke in a panic, my heartbeat synchronized to the exact rhythm of the marching men. Until I was in my teens, that very nightmare would manifest itself each time I was to undergo surgery.

•

Vowing that I would not go back to the hospital ever again, my five-year-old logic formed a plan. "I know what I'll do! I'll run away to my Grampy Gillespie's house. He won't make me go to that awful place anymore."

I found the little white suitcase with the pink satin lining — the one that belonged to me when I stayed in hospital. I packed Cocoa, my prettiest dress, a pair of pyjamas, and a random selection of clothes from the bedroom closet. Carrying the little suitcase with both hands, I edged my way down the winding staircase of our two-storey house — and out the door I went.

Sobbing, I walked down the streets of Grand Falls and tried to remember the direction in which my family had traveled so many times before. The sun was too bright, and with my failing vision it was difficult to see. At last, I came to a railway crossing. "Now where do I go? There are three or four tracks here. Which one do I cross?"

Shifting the weight of the suitcase, I considered my dilemma. Just then, a car pulled up. It was my father, who had been following me the whole time. "Mom misses you, Cheryl," he coaxed from the open window. "You don't want her to be sad, do you? Please, come back home." It was over.

The attempt to escape the monsters of my childhood had come to an abrupt end.

Chapter 6
STARTING SCHOOL

All the children in Victoria County began school on a hot and hazy morning in mid-August. I wore my favourite dress, the one with the puffy sleeves, and a pair of new gold-buckled shoes. "Well, don't you look sweet!" my mother beamed, tying the last pink hair-bobble in my blonde pigtails.

Then came a knock at the door. "Right on time," she said, and welcomed a neighbouring young girl who would accompany me to school.

"Have fun today!" Mom called out, watching her five-year-old daughter walk gingerly down the street.

At noontime, over a bowl of chicken noodle soup, I excitedly told Mom all about my morning recess, and skipping rope on the playground with the other kids. She was pleased to know that I had so quickly made new friends. She listened attentively to the happy tales of school.

But soon, I would run home to her with tears in my eyes.

One day, the teacher, Mrs. Crabtree, called on a few children to stand beside their desks and tell the class a story about a picture from their school workbook. "Cheryl, will you please tell us your story?" I stood, holding the book inches from my face and stared at the page. All I could make out was an image drawn in light grey tones that blended into the beige background. After a long silence, Mrs. Crabtree scolded, "Cheryl, tell us a story, or you will go stand in the corner."

"I can't see the picture," I revealed in a soft voice. "Well, it's a picture of children feeding ducks," she spoke sternly. Mortified in front of all the other kids, I muttered a few words on what the teacher had described and then sat down.

Just like those times when poked by stinging needles, I tightened my fingers into a fist, bit my lower lip, and tried not to cry. Why did this hurt so much? I couldn't ignore the snickering whispers which murmured through the classroom behind me. Then, I fixed my eyes on the long blackboard a few feet away from my desk. The teacher's hen-scratchings were simply a blur. I worried. What if I were called upon again to answer another question?

After one month had passed, school was out for the two weeks of the potato harvest. With a thriving farming community surrounding the town of Grand Falls, many of the older kids spent time working in the fields of their family farm. When the break was over, I did not return to school. Once again, I needed more surgery at the Montreal Children's Hospital.

•

During the extensive period in which I was unable to attend school, Mom took on the role of teacher. Like all children, I loved to colour and draw pictures. Using a marker, she patiently darkened the lines to make it clearer for me to see for colouring and made the numbers stand out for connect-the-dot activities. I also learned to tell time using a toy clock with its large numbers and movable plastic hands.

Spelling words was made fun and easy — with magnetic letters that would stick to the refrigerator. Hanging on our dining-room wall was my very own chalkboard, smaller than the one at school, but when I stood close up, I could see to practice my printing skills. Simple math equations were demonstrated with objects at the kitchen table. "Seven spoons, take away three spoons, equals four spoons."

•

In the springtime, after another flare of arthritis, my muscles had again weakened. Mom had set up a daybed in the living-room, in order to keep me close by while I recovered at home. This was where *Sesame Street* provided hours of entertainment, but I especially gravitated toward gazing through a nearby window, watching the neighbourhood children who played outside.

"Mummy!" I called out, on what seemed to be a particularly long Saturday afternoon.

She appeared in the doorway, wearing her green and yellow checkered apron.

"Yes, Cheryl?"

"What time is it?"

"It's ten past three," Mom answered, noting that she had been summoned to the living-room several times within the hour. "Alright then," she said with encouragement. "Let's get you up and practice a bit of walking."

Carrying me from the bed, Mom stood me next to a wooden chair. Still wobbly, I held on to the furniture and, in small strides, walked from the chair to the end table, then to the sofa, and finally made my way across the room.

"Good for you!" Mom cheered. "You are getting stronger every day! Now, come to the kitchen with me," she said. "I'm baking Johnny Cakes, one of Daddy's favourites!"

Sitting on the floor, I scooted along to the kitchen after my mother. Having weathered three arthritis episodes, the family had become well acquainted with my irregular habits of getting around. Thinking back, Mom related to me how Thom's own first steps had been somewhat delayed, as he had mimicked the actions of his older sister.

While I played with my toy stove, Mom poured the cornmeal batter into a pan. Sliding it into the oven, she set the timer for thirty-five minutes.

"Perfect," she said with a nod and a smile. "It will be ready by the time the children wake from their nap."

Just as my mother lifted the mixing bowl into the sink, a frightening crash was heard. She raced out of the kitchen to the living-room, in time to see a baseball, which the kids in the next yard had hit through the front window, rebounding from the wall. A chill went down her spine when she saw shattered glass in the daybed where I had been only moments ago. Below the window, a neighbouring mother suddenly came into view, rattled at the thought that I might be hurt.

"She's fine," Mom calmed the woman. "Cheryl was safe with me in the kitchen."

Grabbing a broom, Mom began to clean up the broken pieces of glass. She worried what the landlord might have to say about this unfortunate incident. Careful not to miss any small fragments, she swept around a pile of empty boxes soon to be filled with our household possessions, as Dad had recently learned that NB Power would be transferring us seventy miles from our hometown.

•

On Grafton Hill, in the community of Woodstock, is where I recall my fondest childhood memories. There, couples like Mom and Dad had young, growing families. With so many kids in the neighbourhood, my siblings and I liked to stay outside all day, playing Mother May I, Red Rover, Hide and Seek, or Simon Says.

At dusk, Mom would call us inside. Somehow, she made it appear as light work, even though her hands were full with four baths, four pairs of pyjamas, four snacks, and story requests from us four kids. Then it was off to bed, where, after a day of fresh air, we'd sleep soundly till morning.

For Mom, children and nature went hand in hand. In fields and roadside ditches, she would take us on excursions to hunt for pussy willows and cattails. Afterward, our newfound treasures would always be displayed in a vase on the kitchen table.

On May Day, we'd collect pretty rocks, buttercups and daisies, arrange them in baskets which Mom had made, and hang them on the neighbours' door handles, ring the doorbells and quickly run away. Then came that hilarious occurrence when Mrs. Mulherin's door unexpectedly flew open. "Aha!" she called to six-year-old Thomas. "I've caught you, now I get to give you a big kiss!"

"Oh no!" he squealed, racing down the driveway with the woman in playful pursuit.

In October, Mom took pleasure in planning a surprise party for Susan and I, as our birthdays were five days apart. There was lots of laughter as we played Pin the Tail on the Donkey, Spin the Bottle, and Musical Chairs. Then came the balloon-breaking contest.

"Hold the balloon straight out in front of you," Mom described the game rules to our delighted guests. "On the count of three, put the balloon on the chair directly behind you, then sit on it. The first one to burst their balloon wins!"

Pop! Bang! The balloons were bursting all around the room. I bounced, rocked, and wiggled, but try as I might, my balloon would not break!

The early arrival of winter brought more fun, sliding down our backyard hill or making snowmen. On one memorable occasion, my mother cleverly sculpted a snow-horse that we could sit on. Dad also built an outdoor rink, installing floodlights around the ice surface. He informed the older boys in the neighbourhood that they could play hockey after dark on the lighted rink, but that the daytime was reserved for the younger kids who were learning to skate.

•

It was nine p.m., and after a long day, Mom placed her timeworn journal on the chrome kitchen table. A soft glow from the overhead lighting spread across the pages as she carefully penned her next entry.

Dear Cecilia:

At last it's quiet. The children had a soothing cup of hot chocolate, a story read to them, and are now snugly tucked into bed. Of course, Susan had to remind everyone to say their prayer, 'As I Lay Me Down to Sleep'. Thomas finished with 'God bless Grampy and Grammy Gillespie and Grandpa and Grandma Goodine.' Listening to their innocent words, I think of my own prayer: *God, help me to make the right decisions by my children, and particularly for Cheryl.*

It's more difficult for me to write — my fingers being cracked and dry from days of lacing and unlacing four pairs of skates, and putting skidoo suits on and off the kids. I'm happy to report, though, that they are having a blast, and even three- year-old Joan has shown off a couple of her twirls.

Children are so resilient! No matter how many times they fall down on the ice, they get right back up and keep trying. I've seen that same spirit in Cheryl — like her somersaults in the warmer months, she is able to roll through all that comes her way and land on her feet.

Tomorrow morning, my parents will be here bright and early. They'll be looking after the kids while we're away. Our suitcases are packed for the trip, as Martin, Cheryl and I, again, are off to Quebec.

•

From the seventh floor of the Montreal Children's Hospital, Mom watched the traffic lights flash amber, red and green. It seemed there was no end to the steady flow of vehicles, and like a busy ant colony, people were hurriedly coming and going in all directions. Hailing from the peaceful countryside, Mom could have never predicted her life would become as chaotic as the bustling scene below.

"I can't believe we are here for the eleventh time this year," she sighed, weary.

Picking Cocoa up from the nightstand, she quietly tucked him in beside me as I slept. The caramel teddy bear also wore a hospital bracelet reading 'Room 731-A,' a careful measure to insure his safe return in the event that he became lost.

As a mother of a chronically-ill child, Mom kept her composure and, for my sake, learned to conceal her many worries. She understood that maintaining some type of familiar routine, like reading fairy tales as we would have done together at home, made me less fretful. For that reason, Mom and Dad had purchased more books from the hospital gift shop. I loved to hear the stories of *Mr. Grabbit, The Rabbit* by Virginia Hoff, and *Green Eggs and Ham* by Dr. Seuss.

On the other side of my hospital bed, Dad sat quietly, intently holding my hand. He felt powerless to protect his little girl from the phantom thieves which threatened my vision. As well as uveitis, I had developed cataracts and glaucoma. For every operation to treat one eye disease, it ultimately triggered inflammation of another eye condition, and so this battle continued to be a relentless plague.

Unlike most couples in their twenties, my parents were forced to make unpleasant decisions. On our numerous trips to Montreal, they often had no choice but to leave me behind, as I would be admitted for weeks at a time. Despite their struggles, Mom and Dad were comforted in the hospital staff's efforts to bring positive experiences to the sick children. Each weekday morning, from ten until noon, kids could go to the playroom, where the "Play Lady" let them try their hand at painting and crafts which the children would proudly display over their beds.

To Mummy and Daddy,

From Cheryl Louise, age five

Here I am sitting in the playroom in a nice pink chair— and I have pink pyjamas on, and yes, I'm wearing my Lassie slippers — and they match everything. They are a little bit torn because one of the kids tore them by mistake.

I ate all my dinner tonight. I ate fish, potatoes, carrots, milk and three flavoured ice cream. I also had cake which I put in the ice cream - and it's good like that.

Thank you for the books and all my nice cards and especially letters which I'm showing to everyone - my cards are by my bed.

Give lots of love and hugs and kisses to Susan, Tommy, Joanie, Grampy and Grammy Gillespie and Grandpa and Grandma Goodine - and of course to my Mummy and Daddy.

XOXOX

She is a very good, sweet little girl.

~Phyllis Bailey - Volunteer Play Lady.

AUTHOR'S NOTE:

Yes, I can visualize that scene at the Montreal Children's Hospital. And although I did not like fish, carrots, or even ice cream as a child, this was truly a lovely gesture, an endeavour on behalf of the Play Lady to nurture a vital connection with my parents.

•

On Sunday afternoons, patients and their visiting families were often invited to a large room where everyone enjoyed a presentation of a Walt Disney film.

At last, I began to awaken. "Hello, sleepyhead. Dad and I are both here."

"I don't feel good!"

With a steady hand, my father held a cup of ginger ale, the straw close to my lips.

"Okay, just take a small sip," he said. "There. That should settle your stomach."

Hesitating, Mom patted my arm, saying, "We'll need to go soon."

"Why! I don't want you to go!"

"It's getting late, Cheryl. We have to return to the hotel for supper, and get some rest."

"No!" I whined groggily. "You're gonna leave me!"

This was upsetting for my mother. How could she reassure her seven-year-old? Intuitively, she removed the watch from her wrist and placed it in my hand.

"We aren't going home without you, Cheryl. Here, will you keep this safe for me until we come back tomorrow?"

As Mom and Dad kissed me goodnight, I whispered to Cocoa, "Mummy is coming back." Wrapping my mother's keepsake around Cocoa's arm, I tightly hugged the teddy bear, and rested contentedly throughout the night.

•

When we returned to Woodstock, Mom busily prepared all the Christmas goodies. Ever hopeful, we kids hung around waiting to sample the mocha cakes, the shortbread cookies that she cut into stars and the doughnut balls shaped like snowmen. Meanwhile, we listened over and over to the songs and stories from our favourite Christmas record, "Rudolph, the Red-Nosed Reindeer."

In our cozy kitchen, I inhaled the aroma of Mom's Christmas baking. Through a nearby window was an enchanting view of the winter night sky, and the full moon reflected off the sparkling snow. I thought about the previous summer — standing in the driveway with my father and how close the moon appeared to be.

"Daddy, can you lift me up on your shoulders, so I can touch the moon? Please Daddy!"

A wiry young man, Dad obliged, effortlessly lifting me up on his shoulders. I reached my hand as high as I could, but still could not touch the moon.

"Daddy, I bet if you put me up in that tree I could touch it."

"I know it looks close," he explained, "but the moon is thousands of miles away."

The winter scene outside our kitchen window stirred up my imagination. "I wonder what Santa will bring this year? How will he get into our house without a chimney?" Hearing the enthusiasm of the boys playing hockey outside on our rink, my mind turned from fantasy to the reality of my own childhood. "I wish I could run, jump or skate the way they do. What's it like to see what they can see? When will I be able to go to school like the other kids my age?"

•

The day finally came when I could go back to school. It was February 2, one and a half years since that short month when I first attended school in Grand Falls. Mom and I were so excited that we scarcely slept the night before.

Beginning Grade One for the second time was bittersweet. I was eager to learn, yet more and more my vision was diminishing.

"What is the golden rule, class?" The question was asked each morning by Mrs. Shaw, the adored Grade One teacher.

"Do unto others, as you would have them do unto you," the children recited in unison.

An unforgettable lady in my day was Mrs. Betts, a trained nurse and the wife of the school principal, who understood the challenges I faced. One day, Mrs. Betts brought a gift to school that she had created specifically for me. She had designed a wall hanging with a clown face at the top, feet at the bottom, and four pockets in the middle. Each pocket contained flash cards made of bright yellow construction paper, on which Mrs. Betts printed in very large letters new words for me to learn, such as, "HOME," "TRAIN," or "FISH." I was quick to grasp the spelling and reading of words, as my mother had been an excellent teacher during the long absence from school.

•

Two weeks passed. Mom stood at the porch window, satisfied to see that the neighbourhood children were now lining up in her driveway. On one overcast day, Mom had witnessed me drop my lunch bucket as I stumbled on the snow-covered hillside and slammed into a thorny bush that broke my fall. Being a protective mother, she decided to take matters into her own hands — initiating a convincing call to the school district office. As a result, children no longer had to walk down that steep, slippery hill to catch the school bus.

Though I was back in school, it was Mom who continued to have the greatest influence on my early education. In acknowledgement, Mrs. Shaw and Mrs. Betts extended an invitation, asking her to come and observe me in my Grade One class. Mom accepted, although with some apprehension.

"How will Cheryl react to my presence? What if she becomes uncomfortable or embarrassed?"

Not wishing to attract attention, Mom sat inconspicuously at the back of the classroom. Featured throughout the room was an array of decorative shamrocks that the children had made in celebration of St. Patrick's Day. Then, she spotted me, wearing the green barrettes that she had pinned into my hair for the occasion. Mom watched as I leaned forward, showing my best effort to print between the lines which she had darkened for me in the scribbler. I was attentive, with a hunger to achieve, and even before coming to the school, Mom had had every confidence I would be an exemplary student.

At home that afternoon, my mother spread mint-green icing on the cookies that she had baked, suitably cut into shapes of four-leaf clovers. She still worried I might have been uneasy with her in attendance that morning.

"Maybe these tasty treats will do the trick?"

Her doubts were immediately dispelled when, after school, I declared, "Mummy, you looked pretty today!"

It would take extra time to catch up to the other kids in my class, having started school very late that year.

During the summer, Mom sat with me, listening to my reading aloud the stories of Dick, Jane, and Sally from the school reader. When the page became blurry and I could no longer focus my eyes on the words, Mom would read the story's questions, then circle the answers that I had given. Together, all our hard work paid off, and I successfully entered Grade Two in the fall.

•

My new classroom at the Woodstock Centennial Elementary School was warm and cheerful for all the Grade Two children. I especially enjoyed attending music class. There, we listened to each unique instrument, artfully identifying all the characters from the recording of "Peter and the Wolf." I also loved the songs that we were taught to sing, like "Oh Little Playmate," which I gladly performed for my mother after school.

•

Mom had come to recognize a pattern in my chronic illness. Beginning with my diagnosis at the age of two, I would have arthritis setbacks during each of my even years. Now, at eight years old, I would spend weeks in the Woodstock hospital under the care of Dr. Fred Goodine. Fred was a compassionate, old-fashioned doctor who would often make house calls, and was well-loved and respected in the community. Having grown up together in Morrell Siding, my mother admired and trusted her cousin who had become our family physician.

Our last year in Woodstock held more uncertainties. Paying regular visits to our home, Dr. Goodine attended to Mom, who had also become quite ill, due in extent to her overwhelming stress. As for myself, numerous hospital stays were required for active arthritis as well as for eye surgery. Grade Two would not be completed, and soon, news that Dad's work would have our family transferred, this time, to Fredericton.

Chapter 7
A HEARTRENDING DECISION

It was 8:15 a.m. when Dad pulled into the driveway after his midnight shift. He had come home with just enough time to see Thomas and Susan head off to school, make a hasty change of clothes, then promise my mother, "I will be back with Cheryl this evening."

On this late-September morning, my father noticed that the leaves had already turned to the crimson and flaming yellows of autumn. While travelling across the Princess Margaret Bridge, he spotted a flock of ducks paddling on the mirror-like Wolastoq-Saint John River which gleamed under the radiant sunshine. He had less than thirty minutes to make it to the Fredericton Airport where he would catch a flight for Montreal, to pick me up for the final time.

•

Landing at the Dorval Airport, Dad boarded a charter bus which would drop him off near the hotel where he and Mom had stayed on previous occasions. From this stop, he would walk just a few more blocks before arriving at the hospital.

Shoved inside his coat pocket were two plane tickets which he had purchased for the 7 p.m. flight to Fredericton. If past experience were any indication, it seemed wise to book later as we were often delayed while waiting for the doctors to make their hospital rounds and sign the discharge papers.

As Dad entered my room, he smiled at what he saw. There I was, all dressed, sitting on my bed and holding Cocoa. At the foot of the bed, my little white suitcase was all packed. Just then, a nurse hurried in, informing Dad that the discharge papers had been signed and that I was ready to go home. He picked up the suitcase, courteously thanked the dedicated nurses at the front desk, and together we walked hand in hand out of the Montreal Children's Hospital.

Certain that there was an earlier scheduled flight to Fredericton, my father quickly hailed a cab to take us back to the Dorval Airport where he requested to be put on stand-by. As the last two passengers boarding the small plane, Dad and I sat at the very back — the roar of the engines on either side of us. Looking into the infinite sky, my father contemplated the rough journey I had endured, and wondered what would become of his daughter now.

At 3 p.m., much earlier than my mother had expected, Dad and I triumphantly opened the front door, calling out, "Mom! We're home!"

•

With Thomas and Susan going to school, my youngest sister and I had a lot of time to spend together. After playing on our swing set, Joan and I would venture into the backyard woods to collect crunchy leaves of all shapes, sizes and colours. Oftentimes, Mom took us to an empty parking lot on our street where Joan pedalled on her little tricycle, and I could freely ride my bicycle without running into cars.

More and more, I began to navigate my environment through hearing and touch, as my eyesight had faded to merely light and dark perception. Over time, my mother had come to the realization that I would no longer see the pictures which she had outlined for me with markers, or that I would ever again have the ability to read large print.

It had become obvious to my parents that I would require special training and education which they were unable to provide for me at home. Once this painful decision was made, they began the process to send me to the School for the Blind, in Halifax, Nova Scotia.

On the night before I was to go away, Mom kept our tradition of reading a few stories at bedtime. From the Children's Bible, we listened in awe, to "Noah and the Ark", and "Jonah and the Whale." "When Cheryl comes home in three weeks," Mom assured us, "I'll read the Story of Christmas to all of you."

•

It was late November when Dad and I once more boarded a plane, this time landing at the Halifax International Airport. When the cab reached the address on University Avenue, we were cordially greeted by the school principal who would be giving us a grand tour of the historic building. As newcomers, we were taken to the boys' industrial and the girls' home economics departments and guided through two gymnasiums, several classrooms, the cafeterias and the large dormitories.

After an extensive tour, it was time for my father to return to New Brunswick. Swallowing hard, he choked back the tears. He leaned down to hug me goodbye, and I desperately clung to him, crying, "No! Daddy! Please, don't leave me here!" With those plaintive words ringing in his ears, it took every ounce of strength for him to walk away. Heavy-hearted, he disappeared down a dark corridor, and agonized, "How can I leave my little girl like this, feeling like she's been abandoned?"

•

I was inconsolable! This was a strange place, and these were strange people. Then there was that loud, reverberating buzzer — which indicated mealtimes or the end of a class. Shy and afraid, I refused to speak to anyone. I did not want to go to school so far from home, and I certainly did not want to eat!

When the evening came, I was chaperoned up two flights of spiral staircases which led to our dormitory. Throughout the room were ten beds. Beside each bed, a wooden chair on which to set our belongings. With so many children gathered in one room, I wished there were somewhere to hide while I changed into my pyjamas. At least in the hospital, a curtain could be drawn around the bed for privacy, but here, the whole dormitory was wide open.

Climbing under the cold covers with Cocoa, I thought about my mother's bedtime stories, of being tucked into my own bed at home, and of the goodnight kisses from Mom and Dad. So as not to be heard, I buried my face into my pillow and hopelessly cried myself to sleep.

The next morning, I was shown to my classroom which had only seven students. I nervously wondered what grade they would place me in. Would I have to start all over? I'd missed most of Grade Two, and if I weren't in the hospital so often, I would have been in Grade Four by now. My mind was satisfied when they revealed, "Cheryl, you will be in the Grade Three class."

During the first week, I was accompanied by other students while learning my way through these unfamiliar surroundings. After that, I was expected to get along, all on my own.

Kara, a girl from Nova Scotia, immediately took me under her wing. Gaining my trust, she was ultimately my first friend — the one whom I felt comfortable speaking to, and the one who showed me around the school.

Located very near to the Junior Residence where I lived, was the Grade Three classroom. At a much farther distance, through a long corridor and up a flight of winding stairs was the nurses' station, where medications were administered after meals and before bedtime. Past this department and down another hallway, was the room where I spent many hours each day with Miss Watson, the school Braille instructor.

Miss Watson was a strict, no-nonsense teacher, whose husky voice made her seem even more intimidating. Sensing my shyness, Miss Watson wasted no time saying, "When you come to my class, Cheryl, you mustn't answer by nodding your head, because like you, I also cannot see." From that time onward, I timidly spoke to my Braille teacher, albeit very quietly, and the rigid Miss Watson developed a soft spot for me.

Using an abacus, my teacher expertly demonstrated the shapes of the Braille alphabet. There were three rows of larger beads at the top, and three rows of smaller beads at the bottom. "One bead is the letter A," she said, guiding my fingers. "Two beads up and down, is B, and two beads side by side, is C." Once I had learned the letter shapes on the larger beads, Miss Watson then began forming the shapes on smaller beads, until my fingers had become sensitive enough to feel the dots of the actual Braille alphabet.

Toward the end of my first three weeks at the School for the Blind, Miss Watson brought in a surprise. "I have a very special present for you," the elderly woman explained. "This has been my doll since I was a little girl, and now, I would like you to have her."

She gently placed the doll in my lap along with a blanket and some baby clothes. Startled, I uttered a faint "Thank you."

Miss Watson warmly continued, "When you awake on Christmas morning, before you even open your eyes, I want you to thank God for all you have. Will you do that, Cheryl?"

"Yes," I answered, "I will."

●

Upon waking up Christmas day, I immediately remembered Miss Watson's words, then prayed, "Thank you God for my family and for bringing me home. But... please, God, could you send a miracle — and let me stay?"

It was 5:30 a.m. when I heard the crinkle of tinfoil being wrapped over the Christmas turkey. Then, Susan jumped from the bed next to me and hurried to wake the others.

What fun it was that morning, when I discovered Santa had delivered an electric organ for me. On its lefthand side were six buttons. I pressed them, listening to each sound of the major and minor chords. On the right were the keys in which to perform the melodies. Eager to learn, I asked my mother to read from the (play by numbers) music book that came with the organ.

"Okay," she said. "With your left hand hold down the C-chord. And with your right hand count the keys and play, five, six, five, three." Oh! How thrilled I was to hear the opening phrase of "Silent Night."

•

When I returned to the school in January, I was instructed on how to write with a Perkins Brailler. I soon discovered that Braille used contractions to make it quick and easy to read and write. If a sentence was written, "Y C D X," it meant, "You can do it." If I read, "YR FR ALW," it was short for, "Your friend always." I was amazed! In just three months, I would effectively learn the entire Braille Code and thoroughly memorize hundreds of contractions.

•

In Fredericton, my mother turned the page of her kitchen calendar to June. "Finally!" she declared. Mom peered into the living-room, where, as if to usher in the long-awaited month, rays of sunlight now danced buoyantly through the bay window.

Opening a desk drawer she pulled out the family photo album. Leafing through its pages, Mom came upon
our baby pictures. Joan, born just before Christmas, had grown to be a good-humoured five-year-old. Six-year-old Susan, who had dark hair and dark eyes as a baby, was named after the flower, Black-Eyed Susan. Then there was

the fair-haired Thomas, a sensitive seven-year-old boy who had become an avid sports fan, just like his father.

"Oh, there she is..."

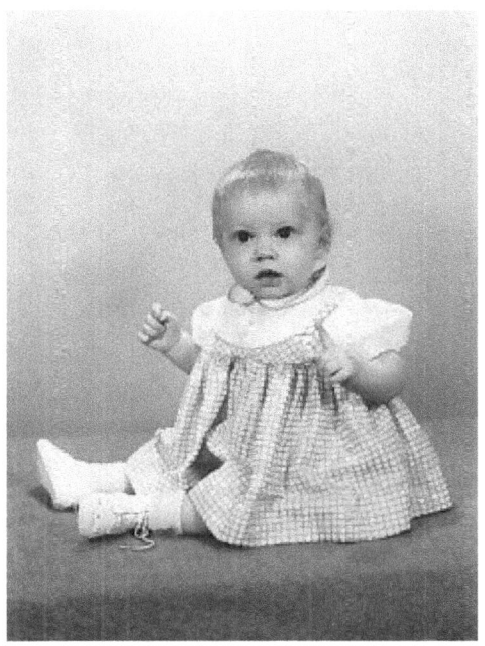

Mom stared at my baby picture. If only she could blot out the memory of my tearful cries when in January, a flight attendant whisked me away, and a I was escorted on to the plane, destined for Halifax. As the holidays had drawn to an end, she recalled my pleading, "Do I really have to go back, Mom? I will never be able to read braille the same way that I could read in print."

Perhaps her answer was meant to persuade both of us. "Yes, Cheryl," she replied, "trust me. You will be able to read Braille, even better than you could read before."

Learning that I had indeed mastered the braille system was encouraging news for my mother. Still, the three hundred miles that separated us might just as well have been a light-year, and the past six months — an eternity.

Setting the album aside, she rummaged through the drawer for her red fountain pen. "June twenty-third," she proclaimed aloud, circling the date on the calendar, as at last, this was the time when I would be coming home for the summer.

Chapter 8
SUMMER VACATION

HOME: a word which conjures up a sense of security, a place of comfort and acceptance. It's not as though I believed we were a perfect, model family, but we did share some pretty incredible memories. Indeed, those were the times which got me through the months while I was away in Halifax.

Without a doubt, summertime was an endless hurrah of recreation for us Gillespie kids! If we weren't flying kites or playing hopscotch, then there was more fun to be had while we raced through the sprinkler, or splashed each other in our inflatable pool.

To our delight, Mom appeared in the backyard carrying a tray of homemade grape, cherry, and lime popsicles. "Which kind would you like," she asked, having recited the three choices to me.

"I'll take pineapple," I answered in jest. "Silly girl! There's no pineapple here." I grinned. "In that case, I'll take lime!"

•

One of our favourite pastimes was exploring the backyard woods. With the notion of being pilgrims, my siblings and I would invent our own secret camp, with fallen leafy branches for walls, and a carpet of moss as the floor. Tree stumps were ideal for chairs, and Mom gladly supplied pie tins from home for our imaginary cookouts.

Before sunset, Mom would call us in for our evening baths. After all, half the fun of childhood adventures was getting dirty, as each day we'd walked barefoot, clearly oblivious to the scorching heat.

A highpoint of summer was visiting our families back in Gillespie Settlement and Morrell Siding. Having grown accustomed to airplanes, I queried, "Why can't we just fly?" I prompted my parents, noting that we would save a lot of time on the two and a half hour road trip!

•

"Are we there yet?" Joan peeked out the window, as the picturesque scene of Gillespie Settlement came into view.

Row upon row of potato plants stood boldly, flaunting their rich green foliage and pink or white blossoms. Next, an array of rectangular canola fields garnished in vivid yellow, appeared like huge slices of bread, each served with a generous helping of mustard. Past the little brook bubbling and swirling into the tranquil lake, we finally drove up that long-anticipated hill leading to the old homestead.

Eager to see our grandparents, we scrambled out of the car and hurried into the large, two-storey house. My father lingered behind, taking in the wide-open spaces spread over one hundred acres of farmland. He remembered working in these fields, rendering everything from the irrigation to the digging of the crops. It was rewarding labour when the two potato houses on the estate were filled to capacity, each containing twenty thousand barrels of the harvest.

A few feet away, the aged, lonely barn where he had milked the cows and fed the chickens, now stood quiet and empty. In the garage connected to the house, Dad smiled as he saw his father's Oldsmobile parked at a slight angle. The garage, once a woodshed, was where he had chopped and piled the wood to stoke the furnace and old stoves in their home.

Dad's trip down memory lane came to a hasty end when his brother Marshall, who lived nearby, drove in with a car full of kids. Soon there would be a flurry of activity as our high-spirited cousins and my siblings happily chased each other around the farm.

It's hard to admit, but I felt somewhat left out while hearing their rambunctious hijinks. All the same, I would never have traded those cherished moments spent with my grandfather.

"Don't we make a fine pair?" he mused as we strolled outside together. "You have arthritis and can't see, and I walk with a limp."

"What happened to your leg, Grampy?"

"Oh, well," he began slowly. "When I was seventeen, I had a wagon load of logs which were hauled by a team of horses. Those back dirt roads are quite bumpy, and when I fell from the wagon to the ground, the wheel ran over me and broke my hip."

Longing to hear more about the past, I asked, "Will you tell me a story about Dad when he was a little boy?"

"I have recollections of an incident when your father was eleven years old," he said with a chuckle. "He walked to the Wright's homestead to go for a ride on their donkey. The burro took him only a little ways before throwing him off. Down the hill he rolled, and straight into the lake with a big splash!" Giggling, I pictured Dad as a boy, soaked from head to toe!

Giving my hand a warm squeeze, he posed, "Well now, let's you and I rest a spell."

Swinging with my grandfather on the front veranda, I was keen to hear more about the old days. "Grampy, why do we call it Gillespie Settlement?"

"As a matter of fact, it was the Wright's who were here first. Then the Gillespie's and other families put down roots and made it their home. The settlement didn't have an official title until the passing of my grandfather, Frank."

The white-haired man's voice began to drift as he reminisced of days gone by. "Frank's daughter and two sons, who were your great aunt and uncles, inherited his house across from the lake, where they ran the local post office. They earned $200 per year, a lot of money back then. Everyone's mail was addressed as being 'At Gillespie', which, my dear girl, is how all these farmlands in the settlement became known by our name."

•

Later that week, the homestead proved even more energetic when my American cousins arrived with their minibikes in tow. My ponytail streaming out behind me, I held on tightly to Dad as he took me for a spin down the Gillespie Road.

My father had often told stories of sliding down this sloped route on his way to school during wintertime. In the middle of the one-room schoolhouse was a pot belly stove under which the kids would set their mittens to dry. Then, after school, he would stop into his great Aunt Alice's house, who always had molasses cookies just out of the oven to give away.

•

Although my siblings were staying at our cousin's house, I, having been gone for so long, preferred to be close to my mother at the farm. Besides, just like in Fredericton, I could easily get around our ancestral home on my own. As for Mom, relaxation was merely a luxury, as she diligently helped Grammy with the household chores.

"We are going to need more veggies for tomorrow's dinner," Mom announced.

It wasn't uncommon for Grampy to take us kids on a trip to the corner store or to the "Five and Dime" in Grand Falls. But on this day, Grampy and I were sent on an errand to the local vegetable stand in Tilley. Upon our return, we would stem strawberries and snap string beans together in preparation for the following day's feast.

On Sunday, the kitchen of the old farmhouse was a gathering place with plenty of food and hospitality to go around. Relatives, neighbours, and even Father Berard, the parish priest who had dropped in for the midday meal, would be seated at the extended table. It made for a very long day, but my Gillespie grandparents treated everyone like family, and they delighted in people stopping by throughout the afternoon.

The day came in late July when Dad, Mom and us four kids would leave the settlement and continue on our journey to Morrell Siding. Standing on the front veranda, Grampy and Grammy Gillespie waved farewell as they watched our green Pontiac depart down that remote country road.

•

Sitting on Grandma's picnic table, I listened intently to each distinctive sound in the peaceful valley. Just over the fence was a field where honeybees droned in a low hum, and nearby treetops gently swayed to the caressing wind. The stirring, wild call of the white-throated sparrow caught my attention with its sweet "Sam-Peabody-dee-dee-dee" song, as if to say "Come-play-with-me-me-me." A short distance away, I overheard an exchange of conversation taking place between Grandma Goodine and my mother.

"Yes, Mama, Cheryl has really progressed in her braille studies. She's even brought a book home to practice her reading this summer."

"Isn't it remarkable how things happen?" my grandmother observed, as the two women continued to wander up and down the rows of the beautifully flourishing garden. "It brings to mind when you were an infant and you had a cyst on your left eye. Our local doctor said that if it didn't go away, he would have to perform surgery. Your grandmother Goodine was very insistent, saying 'That butcher isn't getting near that little face! If she needs surgery we will take her to Montreal.' And do you remember as a toddler, the time that you played outside and were cut below your eyebrow and got an eye full of sand? Twice your sight was threatened, yet now it is Cheryl who can't see."

"Life, it certainly has its twists, doesn't it?" my mother pondered aloud.

"Well ain't that the truth." Grandma then continued, "You know, I believe God spared your sight for a reason!"

•

During the evening meal, Grandma dished up scallop potatoes and homemade baked beans, along with fresh brown bread. It was easy for everyone to work up an appetite, as her kitchen was always a tantalizing potpourri of dill, savory and cloves of garlic.

At the Goodine household, children were expected to eat quietly while the grown-ups talked amongst themselves. Just then, a cow in the pasture let out an enormous, lengthy burp! That did it! All suppertime order was lost to our spontaneous laughter. "Okay, that's enough," Grandma said, trying to hide her amusement.

"But the cow didn't even excuse herself," Joan chimed in, followed by another outburst of tee-heeing.

The next day, Mom's brother, four sisters and their children came together for a Goodine family reunion. Many enjoyed playing horseshoes on a long stretch of lawn, while others danced to fiddle music resounding from the outdoor speaker. "What beautiful hair," Grandpa Goodine said, brushing his hand smoothly down my back as he picked me up in his arms for a brief waltz.

•

On our return to Fredericton, more activities awaited us. We had afternoon picnics, swims at Killarney Lake, and evenings when we roasted marshmallows on the backyard barbecue. One night, we wore our pyjamas, piled into the car and at the drive-in theatre, we watched *The Apple Dumpling Gang* on the big screen. Then all too quickly, summer drew to a close.

Now, conspicuous in the living-room, stood the large blue metallic steamer trunk which would be packed for my trip to Halifax. Clothing for every season was provided, and Mom painstakingly sewed name tags inside each garment — down to the last sock. It seemed not so long ago that I had come home for the summer. In these few days that we had left together, a sadness loomed over the entire family, as once again we would have to say goodbye.

Chapter 9
WORLDS APART

I took the last sweater from the trunk which Mom had so carefully packed, hugging it softly to my face. After drinking in the fading smells of home, I placed the sweater into my dormitory locker. Time and distance had already begun to make summer seem like a far-off dream. Sinking onto my bed, I thought of the long months ahead I would spend away from my family. I worried — what if I forget what they sound like?

In the new residence, I shared a dormitory with five other girls. Across the dorm, a lonesome roommate was being consoled by a houseparent. "Don't cry," she said, the timbre in her speech resembling that of a stick-woman. "You'll be okay." To me, those words rang hollow. How could she possibly know what it was like for a ten-year-old to be so far from home?

At 7 a.m., the houseparents appeared in each dorm making as much noise as possible to awaken us. "Rise and shine," they'd announce with a little too much cheer, while others would cup their hand to their mouth, hamming up their own bugle rendition of the *First Call*. "Urgh," I groaned. "Is that really necessary?"

Before getting up, I wiggled my fingers and flexed my wrists and ankles to alleviate the morning stiffness. Fending off the constant chill of the building, I dressed quickly, then followed the voices of my schoolmates to one of several bathrooms where I would wash my face and hands. For a little girl with arthritis, the morning routine was an exhausting task. Three flights of stairs would lead down to the cafeteria for breakfast, and again, back up those sixty-eight steps to make my bed and brush my teeth. As the startling buzzer announced that school was in, it was down forty-nine steps and through a lengthy corridor to reach my classroom.

"Excellent! You are reading as if you haven't missed any time from school," praised the fourth-grade teacher, Mrs. Graham.

Studying braille the previous year, meant learning to read all over again from the Grades One and Two "Dick And Jane" books. Worried that I might not keep up with the other kids, I knew I would have to practice my reading skills over the summer. Before going home, I had borrowed from the school's braille library a book entitled, *Little House On The Prairie*.

At recess, I stood back and listened with interest to the lineup of students at the money-box. "Are you sure you want to take that much out?" cautioned the houseparent who was recording each individual balance in a book. It occurred to me that the kids who over-indulged would surely run out of money before the end of the school year. Withdrawing 50 cents or more daily from their account, these children then rushed to the school canteen to buy everything, from bubble gum to pieces of liquorish and chocolate bars. Conscientious, I tried not to waste the $20 that my parents had provided for hygiene necessities or for the odd treat.

One day, I decided to splurge on a bag of barbecue potato chips. Hovering too close to me was Raeleen, who hinted, "Oh! Those are my favourite!" Pleased to share, I held the bag out for the girl who greedily thrust her hand in, taking more than half of its contents. Disappointed, I walked away to eat what was left, still pursued by my schoolmate.

"Can I have more?" sputtered the girl with a mouthful of chips.

"I think I gave you enough," I replied nervously, "and I'd like to have the rest for myself."

"You're just being stingy!" said Raeleen with a sneer. This was hurtful, and from that time onward I learned that there were some kids who could not be trusted.

I also witnessed the eager clamour during recess, when parcels wrapped in brown paper and twine or letters from home were distributed to the children. "Dear Theo," a houseparent read aloud for all to hear. "We can't wait for you to come home and meet the new puppy!" Surrounded by the other children, he excitedly opened his package.

"What did you get? Can we have some?" With relentless peer pressure, Theo handed out his goodies to the swarming kids and soon realized he had only one candy left for himself.

Finally, the happy day came when I received my own delivery. Slipping away from the curious throng, I safely tucked the prized possession of Mom's homemade sugar cookies into my dormitory locker. Choosing not to openly reveal the contents of my parcel, that night, I secretly shared a few sweets with those roommates who were not inclined to take advantage of others. When it was quiet, I asked a houseparent to read my letter in private. After all, it was my letter, and was it anyone's concern what my mother wrote to me?

All in all, I was more comfortable living in the intermediate residence than the previous year, when I was under the constant supervision and structure of the junior department. Here, we were allowed to listen to music and play games in the common room, roam the hallways for a casual walk, or spend time in the dormitory surrounded by our personal belongings. We also had permission to venture outside on our own to the playground, where there were swings, slides, a merry-go-round, and ladders to climb up to a deck, where, in my imagination, I was a seafarer on a wooden sailboat.

Keeping the children occupied, especially on weekends, could be a challenge for the residence houseparents. One time, we were delightfully entertained beneath the stars as the houseparents roasted marshmallows over a bonfire in the backyard playground. Other activities might be cookie-baking days in the little kitchenette, or the occasions when we busied ourselves forming clay figures, of which I prided myself on molding little birds and cats. Then there were popcorn nights and creepy ghost stories about the headless watchman, who, it was rumoured, regularly patrolled the school hallways!

Whenever we learned that Pearl was on evening duty as our resident houseparent, we'd hurriedly change into our pyjamas. Sitting in a circle on the floor, everyone would sing along while Pearl strummed her banjo. A favourite chorus that I loved to sing was the beautiful "A Daisy a Day" which conjured fond memories of picking flowers when we lived in Woodstock.

Naturally, we girls on the third floor of the residence would share a common bond and a certain kinship. Still, I never really felt like I had someone I regarded as a life-long friend. Then came Nina, the fun and lighthearted new houseparent.

It was Nina whom I sought out, asking if she would chaperon me to the store whenever I needed more shampoo or toothpaste.

"Well, isn't this a fine predicament," Nina considered aloud as we approached the department store.

"Oh, is it closed?"

"No," my companion explained. "The store entrance has a carousel type booth, but only one of us can get on at a time. I'll go first, then you follow."

The carousel swooshed Nina away. Alone on the sidewalk, I calculated how I might get onto this oversized turntable. With my right hand, I discovered the entrance and its semi-enclosure of three walls, and lifting my foot, I noted that the floor was just a couple of inches from the ground.

"There! I did it!" I breathed a sigh of relief. Then, "What in the world?" I gasped. Realizing that I had spun right back into the chilly November air, I stepped on the carousel once again, this time listening for any sound that might indicate the inside of the building.

"Where did you go!" Nina shrieked.

"Why didn't you tell me when I was in the store?" Reaching for the woman's arm, I sheepishly muttered, "I felt just like my cat — chasing its own tail."

Aware of my distaste for the school cafeteria food, Nina proposed, "Since I'm now off duty, how about we first stop and get something to eat?" For me, this was an invitation I could not refuse.

Seated contentedly in the restaurant, I recounted the dreadful items on the school cafeteria menu: there was the corn beef which surely must have been dipped in the salty Atlantic Ocean; the grainy-textured boiled potatoes with a hint of chlorine; and that unpleasant day they served pizza, topped with hotdogs and carrots! Picking up my fork, I anxiously looked forward to eating something closer to home cooking.

Unsuspecting, I bit on a hard prickly object. In that instant, the fork escaped my fingers and inadvertently landed in my caretaker's lap.

"What was that!" I exclaimed.

"You're all right," Nina assured me, laughing hysterically. "It's just a plastic flower that they put on your plate for decoration."

Regaining my composure, I sighed. "Goodness! What else could possibly happen today!"

•

Now and then, I received a boost of nourishment from the watchful school nurses. "I noticed that you didn't eat your supper," Miss Cameron remarked, as she passed me the evening's medication.

"No," I moped. "I don't like that battered fish and those hard old fries."

"Well, I can't have a picky eater." Miss Cameron invited me to sit while she prepared a slice of toast and poured a glass of orange juice.

Each year, at the first signs of strep throat, I would inevitably spend time in the school infirmary. There, I'd be pampered with chocolate milk, cereal, scrambled eggs, soup and sandwiches. While in the ward, I was also given books and small assignments to work on, like English and math, to prevent falling behind in my school subjects.

•

A dedicated student, there were many things I enjoyed about school. Particularly inspiring was Mr. Moffat's hands-on approach to science. One day, he took us to a local museum where we were granted permission to explore the massive shapes of dinosaur bones and their fossilized footprints. While in our classroom, he'd bring in eggs of baby chicks to hatch in an incubator, and a lifelike muskrat, owl and porcupine preserved by taxidermy which we were free to touch. Then there was that human skeleton from Dalhousie University which he had borrowed in order to demonstrate anatomy.

When the other kids skipped out of their 6:30 p.m. study period, I would find myself alone in this empty classroom. Knowing that I could study better in my dormitory, I resented that my schoolmates had pulled yet another no-show. The harder I tried not to envision Mr. Skeleton standing directly behind my desk, the more my imagination ran wild. What if his bony hand reaches out to grab me? I tried to ignore my superstition but it was no use. I couldn't shake those jitters! Considerably spooked, I gathered my books and swiftly escaped down that deserted corridor.

•

When asked, I was always receptive to helping the resident girls with their homework. In Kara's dormitory, I was coaching her through a math problem when we heard a knock at the door.

"Cheryl, it's time for bed," Nina declared. "Yes, I'll be right there."

As I sauntered down the hall to my room, Nina was there to meet me. "You're seventeen seconds late. Tomorrow night you will go to bed a half hour early." I was puzzled. Why was Nina being so strict? Was she having a bad day? Or, was she trying to make an example out of me so I wouldn't look like her special pet?

Unruffled by Nina's reprimand, I crawled under the covers longing to shake-off the endless chill and dampness of the school. I twirled the loose-fitting mood ring off my finger, and tucked it under my pillow till morning. Besides, nothing could bother me now, with the Holidays just around the corner.

•

Ready for the festivities of Christmas, we children were scarcely able to contain ourselves. It began with the ladies auxiliary annual craft and bake sale. Standing at one of the tables which lined the long hallway, I purchased a small bag of chocolate, vanilla, and mint fudge. Mmm! An irresistible delicacy, I regret to say it lasted only until the next morning.

The following week, the school gymnasium was trimmed for our Christmas party. Although most students had enough vision to enjoy the cheerful decor, more enticing for me was the fresh smell of pine and the mouthwatering scent of cinnamon apple cider. Then, a jolly Santa called each child's name, and one by one, we stepped forward with great anticipation to be presented with a neatly wrapped gift.

•

At the Halifax International Airport, Nina stayed with Theo and I, the two children who were under her care until we were safely on our way home for the holidays. A public announcement had notified travellers that flight 603 departing for Fredericton and Saint John would be delayed due to freezing rain.

An hour passed. Sitting on pins and needles, I waited. "Finally!" I exhaled impatiently as an attendant escorted us on board the plane.

It had seemed like the day would never come when I would be back with Mom, Dad and my three siblings. I longed to feel the warmth of home, and for the delicious aroma of my mother's cooking. I could picture everything. The six-foot Christmas tree, ornamented with a pretty angel sitting at the top, and scattered beneath, gifts from my grandparents which would be anxiously opened on Christmas eve. After watching "A Charlie Brown Christmas", Mom would tuck us snugly into bed, but with all the excitement, it would be hard to go to sleep.

Suddenly, my Christmas daydream was rudely interrupted. "Ladies and gentlemen," the pilot addressed the passengers. "As Fredericton is experiencing a severe winter storm, Flight 603 has been diverted to Montreal. We apologize for any inconvenience. Please fasten your seatbelts while we approach for landing."

In the Dorval Airport, Theo and I sat alone for long, agonizing hours. "I'm getting hungry," complained the boy who'd be travelling onward to Saint John.

"Me too," I replied uneasily.

"Do you have any idea where we are?"

"No." I shifted my weight, as the chair had become extremely uncomfortable. "Hardly anyone walks in our direction. I can't hear a thing — not even if there is a nearby ticket counter."

Isolated and helpless, I wondered why no one came to give us news, offer us food, or ask if we needed to go to the washroom.

At last, we boarded another plane, not to Fredericton, but en route back to Halifax. More than twelve hours earlier I was bursting with elation, but now, I was crushed. Will I ever get home for Christmas?

•

Eerily quiet, the school was all but deserted. Only a few staff members remained, along with Theo and I who had just arrived from our gruelling trip. I was exhausted, hungry, and miserable. Immediately, I was taken to the nurse's department where Miss Cameron provided me with medication, served a hot bowl of soup with crackers, and drew a bath to warm my stiff and painful joints.

"I understand that Fredericton received twenty inches of snow today," the nurse said calmly.

I winced. These were not encouraging words for me to hear. "Don't worry. We've called your mother to let her know you are safe, and that you'll be home tomorrow."

Desperately wanting to believe this gentle nurse, I went to bed, not willing to get my hopes up. Yet, as Miss Cameron had predicted, at 5:00 a.m. I was awakened, relieved to be on my way back home to the family that I had so deeply missed.

Chapter 10
EYE OF THE STORM

Always predictable, "The Arthritis Flare-Up Calendar" was sure to turn a page for me every two years. As each chronic faze ebbed into the distance, I did not brace myself for the next wave. I simply enjoyed life the best way I knew how.

•

It was two days after my twelfth birthday when the children of my residence welcomed the opportunity for a Thanksgiving weekend getaway. A short thirty-minute drive from Halifax, the rustic atmosphere of Miller Lake Camp offered us a primitive sense of adventure with its wood stove, kerosene lamps and outhouses.

In this wilderness setting, the houseparents were in charge of mealtime.

"What would you like for lunch?" Nina asked. "Macaroni and Cheese! Please!" Our voices chanted

in unison.

"Seriously? That's what you want?"

"Yes! We eat it at home, but it's never served in the school cafeteria."

Famished, we devoured every last morsel of a favourite homecooked dish before rushing outside for our afternoon playtime.

•

The October foliage swirled around me as I tossed an armful of leaves into the air. Outmatched by my tumbling leaf fanfare was the woods' own musical cast of overhead creaky branches, the rapid drum roll of a woodpecker and a scolding of a chattering squirrel.

Being away from the school was liberating as Miller Lake imparted a sweet taste of independence. Here, the outdoor surroundings were adapted in that the non-sighted children were able to wander freely throughout the campgrounds. On either side of the cabin's steps, a rope was securely tied to each railing. To the left, a thick cord, running parallel to a wooden walkway, guided us to the outhouses. On the right, I trailed my hand along the rope connected from tree to tree, leading to a short bridge that spanned the nearby brook. As the laughter of kids grew closer, I continued to follow it over a jagged path of rocks and roots, until, with every cautious footstep, I confidently reached the wharf.

It was the boys against the girls, and the canoe challenge was on! Seating ourselves in an orderly fashion, the girls waited to begin their showdown while the slaphappy boys plunged recklessly into their boat. When a whistle gave the signal, the canoes were launched for their brief voyage across the lake. The bumbling antics of the boys made their boat drift in circles but the girls' rhythmic paddle strokes successfully won the race!

•

A few weeks later, we boarded another boat, this time it was the *HMCS Athabaskan*. The tour of this Canadian Navy ship included a brief stop of the torpedo room. While the captain related its varying operations, a resounding beep, beep could be heard as sonar signals were transmitted at regular intervals into the deep waters.

It was a gloomy day of blustering wind and rain when the Athabaskan set sail out of the Halifax harbour and into the choppy Atlantic Ocean. Unable to shake the raw cold, my joints were suddenly gripped with an acute stiffness. "I'll take you to sick bay," a gallant shipmate said before he scooped me up in his arms. "And once you're warmed, I promise to bring you back to your friends."

When I reunited with the rest of the gang, they were already seated in the ship's dining-room for a light snack. Without warning, the cantankerous waves began to surge while the vessel maneuvered back to the docks. A spontaneous laughter erupted from the crewmen as the ship leaned hard, causing their dinner plates to slide aimlessly across the tables. I listened to the mayhem with amusement. That must be why they call this the mess hall!

•

The bitter winter months unfolded, and once more I struggled with a deluge of chronic illnesses. Having a weakened immune system I was more vulnerable to recurring throat infections which contributed to joint inflammation. Thus began my numerous visits to the IWK Children's Hospital. Dr. Peacock, a top physician in paediatric rheumatology was a man of high credentials, charisma and, apparently, good looks. Hanging on his every word, hospital staff seemed to idolize him while nurses shamelessly swooned over their attractive colleague.

From a medical perspective, being under the care of this physician was undoubtedly the right course for my precarious health, yet, at twelve years old, I felt an instant dislike for this egocentric Dr. Peacock. His air of self importance reminded me of one of my mother's old sayings, "There are some men who can't help but strut around like roosters in a hen house."

"She isn't getting any better," he informed the school nurse who had accompanied me to the appointment. "I believe our next course for treatment is to inject her most inflamed joints." By this time I was no stranger to needles, although I shuddered at the notion of becoming a living pincushion.

For once, I wished I were back at the school. Instead, I lay on a hospital stretcher, unable to escape. There were no gestures of comfort for me. All I heard were the giggles of enamoured nurses along with Dr. Peacock's cool, flippant manner while he prepared the shots of freezing and cortisone.

Indifferent to my misery, he inserted the first needle
into my swollen wrist. The pain was excruciating!

"Cry Cheryl, cry!" he taunted. The cadence in his attitude portrayed an image of one with an arrogant smirk. Taking great pleasure in being the centre of attention, the insolent man raised his voice. "I... CAN'T... HEAR... YOU!" He continued to goad, "that a girl — cry louder!"

•

At the school, I stood at the foot of two steep and daunting staircases. Holding tightly to the banister, I strained to take one step, then another.

"What's wrong, Cheryl?" called Nina from behind. Distraught, I opened my mouth, but no words came out. The pain of injections in one wrist and both knees would soon subside, but the hurtful memory of a trained specialist deliberately provoking a child would forever be imprinted on my mind.

In that unspeakable moment, a fountain of bottled-up tears released me of my profound agony. "Shhh," Nina hushed, seeking to console me. "Here, put your arm around my neck and I'll carry you upstairs."

The twenty-six-year-old woman ably gathered me, lumbering up forty-nine steps and through two corridors before reaching my room.

"I didn't think you could do it," I uttered in amazement.

"Me neither," Nina puffed, easing me gently onto the bed. "Now, rest for a bit, and if you need anything, ask one of the kids to find me and I'll come as soon as I can."

●

Shortly afterward, a series of ailments would require another admission to the school infirmary. A bout of throat infections and laryngitis ultimately induced persistent arthritic activity which in turn, led to a painful flare-up of glaucoma.

Attentively, Miss Cameron tucked me snugly into bed. "Cheryl, we have to make you much better before you can go into the hospital for eye surgery." Following a warm bath, I blocked all thoughts from my mind and lazily curled up for a mid morning nap.

No sooner had I relaxed when a whirlwind of Myrtle the cleaning lady barged into the room. I pictured Myrtle as being stout, with untamed bristly hair. The very presence of this woman was frightening, making my joints tense and stiff all over again.

Muttering incessantly, Myrtle spouted words that no one should ever hear, especially children. Covering my head, I hid beneath the bedsheet and waited for her to go away. Her squeaky rubber gloved hands wildly swiped a dust rag across my nightstand. A tissue box knocked violently to the floor, sparked a blue streak of Myrtle's cursing. Then... *Thump! Bang!* With a random swing of her mop slamming into walls and nearby furniture, came another round of her wretched profanity. When Typhoon Myrtle finally blew out of the room as abruptly as she came in, I tried to fathom — the woman must be possessed! How could anyone hire this deranged person to work around kids?

●

With surgery imminent, again I dreamed of sitting in a peaceful, grassy field. Advancing on my quiet solitude were those terrifying armoured men, whose rhythmic marching synchronized with the beating of my own heart. Awakened in a cold sweat, I soon remembered I was lying in a private room of the IWK Children's Hospital.

"I'm here," my mother revealed, giving a squeeze of my hand.

"Mom?" My mind must be playing tricks. "Yes, it's me."

There it was — that familiar warmth in her voice. I then heard the rustle of Mom's down-filled coat as she sat in a chair next to me. She's really here!

"When I received the call about your operation," she began, "I wasn't sure I could come. I told the nurses not to say anything to you — that way you wouldn't get your hopes up."

Prior to this hospital admission, my mother had also learned of the school nurse's attempts to ease my glaucoma headaches. Stubbornly, I refused to drink their prescribed witches brew of Glycerin and orange juice. "Eww! Disgusting!" I grumbled, convinced that the acidic beverage would surely set my stomach on fire.

While Mom endeavoured to distract me from my nervousness, two attendants entered the room bringing unexpected news. "Mrs. Gillespie, we will be transferring Cheryl to another hospital for surgery. She will be returned here again once she is out of recovery."

It was March. An ill-mannered wind blew rudely as they rolled the gurney toward a waiting ambulance.

"Ouch! Stop it! You're hurting me!" I sharply complained to the attendant who had a firm tug on the intravenous pole.

With few exceptions, Mom had been present with me through every medical procedure and treatment. She knew what I had endured and understood why I might be testy, especially when afflicted with the menacing pain of glaucoma.

"Be a good girl." Mom walked along side my stretcher, releasing the tension of the IV line. "I will be right here when you get back. You'll see, things will be much brighter in the morning."

•

Five days passed quickly. In familiar manner, Mom spent many long hours at my hospital bedside, this time reading from *The Adventures of Pinocchio*. We also enjoyed a few rounds of "Snakes and Ladders," a print-braille game which was borrowed from the common room of my school residence.

My health and spirits having dramatically improved, the time had come for Mom to return to Fredericton. As a mother, she was torn. She yearned for more quality time with me, but my siblings, Thomas, Susan and Joan, also needed her undivided attention. Though sorry to leave, she was comforted in the knowledge that she had helped me through yet another difficult ordeal.

•

At the school, Mom glanced around the large room where she had stayed during her time in Halifax. The draughty atmosphere and the dreary walls were particularly unpleasant, and she agreed, the institution's food was horrible! Zipping up her luggage, she slowly walked down the spiral staircase to catch her cab. She hesitated. Looking back at the building, Mom shook her head with a sense of loneliness for her oldest daughter. "No! This is nothing like home. Cheryl doesn't belong here!"

Chapter 11
GOOD 'RIDDINS' TO GOODBYES

"Thank Heavens — it's Friday!" I declared, dropping a mountain of braille books onto my bed. Just when I thought I had caught up on my Grade Eight assignments, Mr. Scott decided that today, Remembrance Day, was the ideal time to give us the weekend to study for a test on World War I. "Bummer!" I groaned, as history was my least favourite subject. Never mind that — my plan is to sleep in tomorrow morning.

Expecting a quiet evening alone, I closed the door to my semi-private room which I shared with Kara. During weekends, she often spent nights in her other friend's dormitory, leaving me to indulge in perfect solitude.

Though sparsely furnished, our small room with its shelves, drawers and lockers, offered sufficient storage for each of us. Next to my bed, the pipes from the radiator spread a desirable warmth, a comfort that I was unable to find in any other part of the school. At the foot of our beds was a wooden desk on which sat a brass lamp, my radio and a stack of assorted print books belonging to Kara.

It just didn't make sense: why was only a quarter of the student population totally blind? Most were not required to learn braille or use white canes, given that they were either colour-blind or had partial sight loss. If that were my situation, I was pretty sure I wouldn't be living in this place.

For me, the months spent away from home would have been dull and empty were it not for the companionship of my radio. How I loved to sing the lyrics to every song, transporting me into a world of my own. Hugging my pillow, I began to sway in an impromptu dance up and down the narrow aisle between the two single beds. Suddenly, a knock at the door ended my Cinderella waltz, bringing it to a lopsided, inelegant pose.

"Are you in there, Cheryl?"

"Um, yes, you can come in," I answered, discreetly placing my pillow back on the bed.

Stepping into the room, Nina calmly informed me, "There is a phone call for you downstairs in the office. It's your mother."

My heart leaped with excitement as I quickly raced down forty-nine steps. I could not imagine why Mom would be calling, especially since my parents had given me permission to telephone home every other Wednesday night.

"Hello, Cheryl," my mother greeted me in a somber tone. "I'm sorry," she paused. "I have some bad news for you."

I was worried. Never before had I heard my mother sound so distraught.

"What is it, Mom?"

"Your uncle Marshall died today."

I sat motionless. "Are you okay, Cheryl?" she asked.

At fourteen years old, this was my first experience with a family death, and I needed to process it several hundred miles away from everyone I cared about. Pressing the phone to my ear, I heard my mother's stifled sobs and her quivering words, "At least we'll always remember him."

Having returned upstairs, once more I shut the door behind me. I felt numb inside, as though my soul were being protected by a veil of winter frost. "Why God?" I lashed out. "How could you take him away from his wife and kids? It's not fair! Why would you let us grieve like this?"

Clinging to Cocoa, a trickle of lonely tears began to flow, dampening the fluff on my teddy bear's head. As the radio played Eric Carmen's "All by Myself", my attention was drawn to a beautiful interlude from Rachmaninoff's piano concerto. For a moment, my crying stopped as I absorbed every note of this haunting melody. Having studied piano over the last two years, I was beginning to appreciate the subtleties of music. Oh! If only I were able to play with such grace.

After midnight, I turned off the radio. All was quiet, except for an occasional creaking inside the building and the mournful wail of the foghorns at the Halifax harbour.

Then, as if in a whisper, a voice told me: *Cheryl, everything will be alright.* Could this be my imagination? Was God trying to communicate some sense of peace? Sliding into bed, I recalled my mother's words, "At least we'll always remember him."

"Oh, that's what she meant," I yawned, "he died on Remembrance Day." Emotionally spent, I closed my eyes and soon fell into a deep sleep.

Each day, I thought about my family and what they might be doing right now. *I wonder what the weather is like in Fredericton? What did Mom make for supper, and was there a chocolate cake for Dad's birthday? How are Thomas, Susan and Joan doing in school?*

Over time, I had become well accustomed to life away from home. Sunday, Tuesday and Friday were designated as bath days for the girls — although I would sneak in an extra bath whenever I could. On Monday we gathered our unwashed clothing and stuffed them into cotton bags to be sent to the laundry department. Wednesday was the day we stripped our beds and made them up with fresh white linens. Then on Thursday, our garments were again returned to the residence and placed in separate folded piles on a table in the kitchenette. Before bedtime, each student would pick up their clean clothes by the armful, and carry them upstairs to be put away.

Along with our academic courses, weekdays were a bustle of extra-curricular activities. In gym class, students could exercise on the floor mats, walk on the balance beam, climb the wall ladders or perform tricks on the giant trampoline. We also looked forward to swimming instructions on Wednesdays, travelling by bus to a city pool. Optimistically, I tried out for the competitive swim team, and although I possessed good technique and endurance, my swim times didn't make the cut.

When the boys went to industrial class to sharpen their skills in mechanics, woodworking and the like, the girls attended home economics class where we'd learned to knit, sew, and dabble in a bit of cooking. As for the music program, while most students participated in choir, the highlight of my week was definitely piano lessons.

On the other hand, weekends had frequently proved to be monotonous and downright boring! If only I were allowed to play the piano! *Shhh!* That was my little secret. Often, I waited until the coast was clear before making my getaway to the music department. It was easy to walk quietly while on the marble-like floor of the long hallway but when I arrived at the wooden ramp, I was careful to avoid those pesky squeaks. From here, I would take a left past the principal's office and up two flights of stairs.

"I know I shouldn't be here," I whispered. First, I checked the door to Mrs. Hubley's music room — it was locked. I then jiggled several doorknobs of about a dozen small practice rooms which were located on either side of the school auditorium. "Aha!" I exclaimed, finally able to enter the seventh room.

Moving the bench to a comfortable position, I sat down and began to play softly, fearing that the music might alert someone and I'd be caught. Soon, my fingers confidently improvised a few popular songs from the radio, along with old tunes I remembered hearing at the Goodine family homestead. Aware that Mrs. Hubley frowned upon such "fooling around" during my weekly practices, this private rendezvous was just the opportunity I needed to spread my musical wings.

Immersed in such melodies, I forgot how ghostly it was in this deserted part of the school. Having lost all track of time, I was astonished when I heard that awful supper- time buzzer. Hastily, I pushed the bench in place, closed the door and scurried back to my residence.

•

April had arrived, and the staff and students were prepared for our annual open house. On this appointed Sunday, the public was invited to attend and observe the children at the school for the blind. Ugh! I hated having to be on display as though I were in some kind of a freak show. Not to mention, our seldom jammed corridors felt like I was dodging a crowd of shoppers during midnight madness as I forced my way from class to class!

It was not a typical day for staff nor students. Everyone was expected to be on their best behaviour, including our geography teacher. Renowned for carrying a yardstick to loudly whack the students' desks, Mr. Grimsby was velvety smooth on this day! After dictating a few paragraphs to the class, he chose a braille student to read for the benefit of our onlookers. I inwardly panicked. *Don't pick me! Please, don't pick me!*

"Theo, would you like to read aloud for us?"

Oh brother! The cranky Mr. Grimsby now resembled

that of a Cheshire cat flashing his superficial grin.

When Mr. Grimsby had finished his dictation, a few bystanders approached me asking if I might write their names into braille. Although bewildered by their fascination, I was relieved to fulfill this request as opposed to reciting some gibberish in front of strangers.

The last class for open house day was in home economics. I enjoyed the creativity of a variety of domestic arts, of cooking, pottery, weaving on a loom, learning to macramé, rug hooking, and most of all, knitting and sewing plush animals.

With precision my fingers guided the sewing needle, pulling the thread through the fuzzy fabric which would soon be made into a stuffed skunk. Ignoring the spectators peering over my shoulder, I smiled, thinking of an incident at home the previous summer.

One night after we had gone to bed, the room that I shared with my sisters became filled with an unmistakable odour. Presumably curious, a mischievous Joan looked outside and carefully placed a toy Sylvester the cat on the window ledge.

"Oh my goodness!" she exclaimed in exaggerated drama. "Susan! The skunk is right outside the window!"

In disbelief, Susan climbed out of bed. Drawing back the curtain, the black and white stuffed culprit lunged forward landing on top of our unsuspecting sister. Her sudden screech immediately brought Mom to the bedroom door.

"What is going on in here?" she demanded.

Giggling, we related the story while Mom held back her laughter. "Alright," she sighed, putting an end to our shenanigans. "Go to sleep!"

Finally, the four o'clock buzzer proclaimed the end of this year's open house. It was time for the roaming visitors to leave and for me to return to the privacy of my room.

•

The arrival of spring also initiated the kick off to our next school event, track and field days. A widespread enthusiasm rallied an atmosphere of competition among the students. Everyone took part in a tug-of-war, the long jump, a ball toss, the three-legged race, among several other contests. Having arthritis meant that I didn't possess the speed nor agility of my competitors, but I always gave it my best shot.

As the girls lined up for the 100-metre race, Raeleen heckled, "Why do you even show up… you never win!"

I had come to expect such snide remarks from Raeleen as I flashed back to her boorish whoops while we rehearsed for majorettes. "You are out of step with the rest of us!" she hollered. Initially, I was excited to join this girls' troop. In the end, being the only totally blind participant and having to endure Raeleen's constant ridicule, I believed I just wasn't good enough.

Kara readily came to my defence. "Don't listen to that mean Raeleen."

I thought of my brother, Thomas, who just last week had shattered a twelve-year New Brunswick provincial record in the four hundred metre race. "Well, I may come in dead last," I conceded to Raeleen, "but I bet you could never beat my brother!"

•

Glints of sunshine poured through my third-floor window hinting at the sweet promise of summer. Even so, I was preoccupied by a telephone conversation I had with my mother nearly three weeks ago.

"Mom," I began, "I want to come home and go to school in Fredericton. I don't want to be here anymore. Will you help me?" I begged. "If I can't go to school at home, I will simply quit!"

A stay-at-home mom for more than a decade, my mother now worked as a cafeteria supervisor in a local junior high school. Knowing how determined I could be, she was not at all fazed by my plea.

"Okay," she agreed reluctantly. "I'll talk to the staff at work, but I think you need to speak to your superintendent," she advised. "Maybe he will give us some guidance. Can you do that?"

Mom's request presented more difficulty than I had anticipated. Numerous times, I approached Mr. Olivier's office, only to lose my courage and hurriedly walk away.

Then there was an uncertainty with Lauren. Yesterday we stood side by side in the girls' bathroom, the one with two toilets, three tubs and a row of five sinks. After brushing her teeth, Lauren surmised, "I guess you are going to school in Fredericton next year?"

"How did you know that?" "Your dad told my dad."

Of course, why didn't I think of this? Lauren was a fellow New Brunswicker and our fathers both worked for NB Power.

"Nothing is settled so please, Lauren, don't say anything to anyone."

She's a nice girl, but could I trust her? Well, that did it!

"I can't put this off any longer," I scolded myself. "I will have to talk to Mr. Olivier tomorrow."

A commotion in the hallway interrupted my deep thoughts. Amongst all the chatter, did I overhear something about an afternoon outing? For the most part, I understood that the houseparents sincerely tried to keep us entertained, but some of their activities left me shaking my head in wonder.

I thought about when we went sliding down Citadel Hill on a winter's day; seemingly a good idea at the time, until my toboggan and I became airborne and landed with a thud! With the wind knocked out of me, I lay still for a moment. A few bruises later, I vowed it would be my last hurtle down this monstrous hill.

In another instance — after tickets had been donated to the school — we found ourselves at the Halifax Metro Centre attending a presentation of The Ice Capades. The figure-eights and triple axels on the ice surface below were met with tremendous applause. But for one who was totally blind, the artistry was impossible to appreciate.

And what about that field trip to Oak Island? There, for two centuries men have searched for treasure, commonly believed to be buried by the infamous Captain Kidd. On a sunny day, we stood in close proximity to deep excavated holes cordoned off by ropes. It may have enthralled the sighted kids, yet for me, this excursion was but a disappointing memory.

Then came that colossal flop, the time we were escorted to a movie theatre where on the big screen was playing, "The Pink Panther." With minimal dialogue in the show, the only thing I remembered taking away from this experience was the reoccurring orchestral theme, "ta-dum, ta-dum!"

Good grief! What would our activity be today? Charades anyone?

Just then, Kara burst into the room. "Cheryl, are you coming?"

"Where are we going?" I remained sceptical.

"To the beach! Get ready! I'll meet you downstairs."

•

It was a beautiful June day, the warmest of the nine months spent in Halifax. Kara, who had enough vision to see road signs and traffic lights, accompanied me on our walk to the beach. On each city block, I breathed in the distinctive perfume of purple and white lilacs, in full bloom at this time of year. Arriving at Point Pleasant Park, we continued on the extensive forest-lined trail of crushed rock before reaching the seashore.

Removing my shoes and socks, I ventured away from the group — keeping an ear on the kids' voices directly behind me, and the ocean waves to the right. Walking barefoot in the sand, I listened intently to the incoming tide and the squawking of seagulls in the distance.

Beneath the afternoon sky, I stood at the water's edge, impressed by the massiveness of the Atlantic Ocean. In what seemed to stretch out forever, I heard a wave gathering strength, then whoosh, it splashed onto my feet. How minuscule I must be in the scheme of things, I thought. Just imagine, there is a God who oversees all of this, the sky, the oceans, the universe, and even a girl like me.

As though wedged in a pedicured massage, I dug into the warm, spongy sand, but soon cringed at the tangled bunches of seaweed. "Eek! What creatures could be living in that?" I uttered squeamishly.

Dipping my toes into the chilly water, I waded in up to my knees. I gaged the rhythm of the incoming tide, steadied myself, and in my own inventive game, jumped over the rushing waves.

Soon, the houseparents rounded us up for our return to the school. By the time I was back in my room — having walked almost eight miles — my joints pained. I was beat! I had to admit, though, this was a good outing after all, and with my mind refreshed I was in better spirits for tomorrow.

•

It was after school on Monday, when I started toward the superintendent's office. I had butterflies in my stomach all over again. "You have to do this," I told myself.

After a timid knock at the door, I heard Mr. Olivier's' cheerful greeting, "Hello Cheryl! This is a pleasant surprise!"

As he led me to a comfortable armchair, my nervousness faded. I wondered why I had made such a fuss, and now thought, surely, he will understand.

After revealing the purpose for my visit, Mr. Olivier firmly replied, "Cheryl, you absolutely cannot do this!"

"Why not?" I took issue with his response.

"You have no idea what it's like out there!" The man spewed his candid remarks. "Public school is extremely difficult, and as a blind student, you'll never make it!"

"I believe I can do it."

"If you insist on going through with this," Mr. Olivier warned, "don't expect any help from us, and I guarantee that we will not supply you with braille books."

I was devastated! It had taken immense courage to come face to face with this man, only to have my hopes dashed. How could he be so cruel!

"There there, Cheryl. I'm sorry I've upset you," he said. "Now, perhaps you should go do one of your favourite hobbies. Maybe try some knitting, and put this whole thing out of your head."

Flustered, I stormed out of Mr. Olivier's' office. Taking the quickest route to my room, I disappeared before anyone would notice the tears streaming down my face.

•

It was the last day of school, before all the students would depart for the summer. With long strokes of the brush, I smoothed out my blond hair which fell clear to my waist. Wearing the dusty rose dress which Mom had sent for the closing ceremony, I proceeded to the school auditorium.

I joined my classmates, then sat beside Kara for our year end celebration. The ceremony began with a performance on the Casavant pipe organ, followed by an opening message of the school superintendent. Striving not to obsess on his hurtful words, I reminded myself that tomorrow, I would be back home.

Throughout the evening, students waited in eagerness for the award's presentation. I had received various commendations during my time at HSB, and, as I recall, this year was no exception. Specifically, after being invited to the stage several times, I remember shrinking into my seat, and thinking, *For goodness sakes! Is he still talking? How long before I can get out of here?*

I had effectively ignored Mr. Olivier's speeches when came one more announcement:

"For the student in the intermediate residence, exhibiting kindness and helpfulness to others, the prize goes to Cheryl Gillespie!"

What! As one who was shy, I couldn't grasp receiving such recognition. During these six years at the school, I had never obtained a prize for residential living, prompting the question — why now?

Walking down the busy corridor, I passed Mr. Olivier surrounded by a boisterous crowd of kids. "Cheryl!" he called out. I hesitated, and turned in the direction of his voice. "That is a beautiful dress you are wearing," he expressed charmingly. "Congratulations on all your prizes. I'll see you in September."

Hmph! A few days ago he was a bully, and now he is flattering me with compliments? I was too angry to speak. In disdain, I spun around and without a word, continued toward my dorm to pack for the trip home.

•

Early next morning, I gathered the few last personal items and placed them into my suitcase. I always looked forward to summer vacations with my family, but this time, the decree passed down by 'His Highness, Sir Olivier' filled me with doubt and sadness. Nevertheless, outside of Lauren, I was thankful my intentions of attending school in Fredericton hadn't been communicated to the other kids. Well, at least my dignity would remain intact.

Certain that I would return to Halifax in the fall, I figured goodbyes were irrelevant. Besides, I hated goodbyes, especially when leaving my family. There was the time when, just before boarding the plane, Thomas wrapped his arms around me, saying "Don't cry, Cheryl. I love you." This sweet attempt to console his older sister made me weep even more.

At last, it was time to go. I tiptoed into the hallway, careful not to wake the sleeping residents. Out of nowhere, I perceived a presence behind me.

"Were you just going to leave without saying goodbye?"

It was Kara. Her tone was somewhat dismayed.

"What? I'll be back in a couple of months," I replied, shrugging off her question.

"No you won't. I know about you going to school at home."

"Oh. I suppose Lauren said something. It doesn't matter what I want, Mr. Olivier won't allow it."

"I know you, Cheryl... you'll find a way. I just want
to say goodbye."

Again, I picked up my suitcase to carry it down two flights of stairs. I turned toward Kara, and replied in resignation, "See you later."

•

Arriving at the hometown airport, my father met me with a welcome bearhug. "I hear you want to go to school in Fredericton," he said cheerfully.

"Well Dad... there's no point in talking about it," I disparaged. "It's not going to happen!"

"Yes it will," he assured me. "All the arrangements have been made. You'll be going to school here, just you wait and see."

I couldn't believe my ears! After spending six years in Halifax, I was suddenly anxious and hopeful at the same time. Just then, my luggage and steamer trunk containing all my worldly possessions arrived on the conveyer belt. Taking my hand in his, Dad exclaimed, "Let's go home, Cheryl!"

Chapter 12
CULTURE SHOCK

When I arrived home in June, I learned that for the first time I would have a room all to myself. Such a luxury, as I had always shared my space whether in Fredericton with my sisters, or in Halifax with multiple roommates. It was perfect! I could arrange everything just as I pleased. Matching outfits were carefully hung together in the closet, while the stuffed skunk which I had made in sewing class, along with a comb, jewellery and radio were neatly placed on the dresser. Cocoa kept his prominent spot, sitting on the bed next to my pillow.

It's always the little things that are treasured most: like the times we'd gather for some family TV while my siblings freely explained the actions on the screen. How natural it had become for them to describe the images to me; even in my absence, they were occasionally known to relate these scenes to the puzzlement of their visiting friends!

Then there were the kittens born to our family cat, Miss Kitty. Soon, all but one from the litter had been given away to good homes. I recall an incident at breakfast when I heard a curious trickling, only to find the remaining kitten lapping up some milk on the other side of my cereal bowl! Giggling, I picked up the tiny ball of fluff. "Frisky! How did you sneak up on the table?"

As cats are known to reduce stress, is there any secret why I've always gravitated toward their purring softness? We were inseparable. Throughout the summer, my furry companions and I could always be found together, a calming outlet while I faced the uncertainties of attending public school in the fall.

•

Under a clear September sky I approached our backyard hammock. This was my chance to savour the last drops of warm sunshine before school was in. On this Labour Day Monday, the streets were quiet, and to my relief, even those pesky grasshoppers hadn't flown nearby to torment me. After all, the sharp, snapping of their wings had me convinced that they must be at least two feet long!

Arms curled behind my head, I reclined and ignored the acidic churning in my stomach. It was no use. The more I tried not to think of tomorrow's entrance into public school, the more it weighed on my mind. I will be the only blind student there. Would I make a fool of myself? What if I fail? My only reassurance was that at the end of the day, I would be able to come home.

I steadied a cup of ice water and took a sip. You can do this! Forget about that stuff, and dwell on the things that make you happy. Still fresh in my mind, I decided to indulge in a few pleasant highlights of the summer. Besides, what could be more peaceful than Morrell Siding?

•

The soft blades of grass felt cool between my toes as I strolled on the front lawn of the Goodine homestead. Resting a moment under a shade tree, I lightly swept my hand over a thick patch of clover. The valley lay still, except for a cheerful chorus of twittering birds, accompanied by an ovation of flapping leaves. I sensed a timeless charm about these rural surroundings, a tapestry of olden days that seemed to weave itself into the present moment. While I imagined what life must have been like for earlier generations, a herd of cattle, heading out to pasture, trundled down the road.

I stood to move away from a cloud of dust, kicked up by the procession of grass seeking cows. Walking toward my grandmother's garden, I stretched out my hand in search of the two pink flamingos which I remembered seeing in early childhood. Then, I reached for the stone sundial that measured about waist high. At the threshold of the garden lay a bed of dahlias and gladiolus, ideal for attracting bees to pollinate. Next I discovered Grandma's old laundry tub; made for a perfect container to plant nasturtiums of bright yellow and orange.

When I felt the packed soil under my feet, I knew that this was the path that would guide me between the rows of vegetables. There were corn stalks standing straight and tall, and peas in the pod that climbed a chicken wire fence, held up with cedar posts. Stakes and garden twine supported the tomato plant, overloaded by its red and green fruit. A little further, I recognized the distinct smells of onion and dill. "Mmm! Rhubarb pie..." My mouth watered as I passed the delectable perennial with their large heart-shaped leaves.

Toward the end of this paradise, I was careful not to step on the pumpkin and squash which had grown from the garden and spilled into the grassy area. I followed their voices, and soon joined my siblings, my mother and grandmother at the picnic table where we all shelled a huge pail of peas to be ready for supper.

•

Suddenly, my countryside reminiscences were distracted by a nearby hissing. "Miss Kitty? Frisky, is that you?" I listened intently, then came another *Hissss!*

I sprang to my feet and hurried into the house. "Mom," I exclaimed. "There's a snake outside!"

"Nonsense! There's no snake out there. Go on, and enjoy the sun while you can."

I cautiously opened the sliding glass door, then stepped on the patio and kept my ears peeled for suspicious sounds. Jitters brushed aside, I allowed my thoughts to stray back to our recent trip to Gillespie Settlement.

"Well well! I hear you're going to school in Fredericton this year." I felt a slight tremor in Grampy Gillespie's hands as he twisted my hair into a braid.

Perhaps it was our physical limitations that gave us that special bond. Whatever it was, I knew my grandfather understood me.

"Yep! It's a bit scary," I told him, "but at least I won't be going away."

"I don't doubt that you can do anything when you put your mind to it."

There was one last tug on my hair. "Okay, I'm done.

Pass me your scrunchie."

I thought I would humour my grandfather when at first he called out, "Come here! Let me braid your hair."

Running my hand down the full length of the braid, I expected to find a tangled mess. It was beautiful! "Wow! How did you do that?"

"Once upon a time, I used to braid the horses' tails." "You're kidding!"

Known to tease, I wasn't sure whether to believe Grampy.

"I sure did," he continued. "It made the horses look tidy, and it helped keep the flies away! Ha ha!" He gave my hand a squeeze. "Well now, your grandmother is in the kitchen. Go on and show her that pretty new braid."

I stopped at the old screen door leading to the front veranda, and eavesdropped on what seemed to be the conversation of the summer.

"You have a smart girl there, Martin," a man's voice said, "but how do you suppose she will make out in public school?"

"Shelia has made all the arrangements. She spoke with the principal, the teachers, and everyone is..."

As I strained to hear the rest of what Dad was saying, a jet from Loring Air Force Base flew over, drowning out his words. Shrugging my shoulders, I went on my way to the kitchen.

"Grammy, look at my braid!"

"Oh, isn't that nice! Did Grampy do that for you?

Come, sit down and have a molasses cookie."

In a tall glass of milk, I dunked one of my grandmother's homemade spicy treats, until it was soft enough to melt in my mouth.

"You know," she began, "I pray every night that someday you'll be able to see again."

It wasn't the first time she had expressed these words to me. No doubt, Grammy was sincere, but now the prayers that had once offered encouragement were really starting to bother me.

Not thinking, I heard myself blurt out, "Grammy, instead of praying that I will get my sight back, why don't you ask God to help me cope with the way I am now."

My chatty grandmother fell momentarily silent. I gulped. Oh-oh! What did I do?

"Cheryl," she confessed, "you're right! I suppose I never thought of it that way."

•

Hissss! Again, that sound jolted me into the present. "Oh stop it!" My body tensed. "Mom said there's no snake. You're imagining things."

"Hey, look!" a boy passing by shouted to his friend. "It's a snake!"

Scrambling out of my hammock, I raced back into the house. "Mom! There's two boys outside who saw it!"

"Saw what?" Mom slid the door open and stood on the patio.

"Boys! What are you doing?" I heard my mother shout. "Alright now. Put the snake down...thank you!"

In the living-room, Mom asked how I could possibly hear a snake, some forty feet away.

"I told you I wasn't imagining things."

"You and your ears," Mom laughed, giving me a playful tap. "If you're staying in, you should go upstairs and pick out your clothes for the morning."

•

By late evening, Mom finally put her feet up. Laying the journal in her lap, she turned several pages, reached for a pen, and began to write.

Dear Cecilia:

It's back to school for the kids, and back to work for me. Reality set in when I was making not three, but four bagged lunches. Oh my! Can you believe it?

Cheryl is going to public school!

We had quite a summer, though. Taking her to a nearby pool, a student instructor helped Cheryl to improve her back stroke, front crawl, and build endurance for treading water. She has earned the standard Junior Red Cross swimming badge, and is now working her way toward the intermediate level.

She's now into mystery books, like "Trixie Belden." More than once, my voice went hoarse while reading these spooky tales to her.

In a good way, these past two months were different. I didn't have that ever-looming feeling of sending Cheryl to Halifax.

Whenever she'd leave, the household just wasn't the same. I think of the nights when Susan would look across the room to see Cheryl's empty bed, and how she cried, feeling scared and lonesome for her big sister.

At mealtimes, it was hard for us to keep from staring at the vacant chair which sat between Thomas and Joan. That is, unless Miss Kitty snuck into Cheryl's spot, where she would peek over the edge of the kitchen table. Such antics would lead to an outbreak of much needed laughter!

As time passed, I worried about the consequences of sending Cheryl away. Would she grow to resent us? What if she became emotionally distant from her family?

There were many sleepless nights, thinking of what fun things the kids and I would record on cassette to mail to Cheryl. I'd rack my brain for a new parcel idea, anything to keep her connected to home.

Six lonely years later, and here we are. If I've learned anything, it's that life is unpredictable. Who knows what tomorrow will bring.

•

As Mom and I walked across the school parking lot, I observed the early morning chill. This was already a new experience for me. After all, in Halifax we had no reason to go outside for school with our residence and classrooms under one roof.

Once inside, I flinched at the surge of boisterous kids. My muscles tightened. The harder I tried not to look awkward, the more I felt like a starched paper doll.

"This is where I work," Mom described the surroundings as we passed the cafeteria. "We're coming up to eight steps, then we'll be in the hallway to your homeroom class."

Threading our way through a congested corridor, I recognized the slamming of metal locker doors. I ducked behind my mother, avoiding the elbows of so many students who were hanging their jackets all at the same time.

Waiting for me was my homeroom teacher. "Good morning, Shelia and Cheryl." Hearing her voice, I guessed the woman stood fairly tall.

"This is Ms. Violett," Mom introduced me, directing my hand to greet the teacher.

"Your mother has told me so much about you." She added, "Now, if I'm not doing this right, just say so," and offering her arm, Ms. Violett led me to the front of the classroom.

Knowing that I was in good hands, Mom called out, "See you later, Cheryl."

There was barely enough space for everything on my desk. I had a three-ringed binder where I would keep notes, the Perkins Braille Writer donated to me by the local Lion's Club, and a cassette machine which I would use to record school sessions.

"Alright everyone! Please say 'here' as I take attendance."

I estimated at least four times as many students than were in my classes in Nova Scotia. How on earth will I remember all their names?

"Let's begin with an overview of our math course this year." I appreciated Ms. Violett's style as she spoke aloud the notes she jotted on the chalkboard.

"We will build on the 'INTEGERS' and 'PRIME FACTORS' that you studied in Grade Eight."

What? I had never heard these terms before!

Over the next few months, it would be necessary to double my efforts in the math course. This meant keeping pace with the new Grade 9 material while catching up on the Grade 8 math concepts that hadn't been covered at the school for the blind. Groan! Mathematics times two!

As the bell rang, I immediately jumped up from my chair, as we had done at the end of a class in Halifax. Apparently I was the only one standing. Detecting all eyes on me, I gave a nervous flip of my hair, and acted as though I were straightening books on my desk. Smooth, Cheryl! Everyone can see that you're not arranging just one binder!

•

That afternoon, Thomas helped me on to the school bus. "Hey Thom! Come sit with us!" Witnessing the popularity of my brother, I wondered how long it would be before I would make friends of my own. Ms. Violett had introduced two girls who would accompany me to each class, Katharine and Tamara. Could it be them?

•

Back home, an inviting aroma of roast chicken wafted throughout our house. "Oh, Mom!" I inhaled. "That smells so good!" I hung my coat in the hall closet, and hurried into the kitchen. Above the warmth of the stove, I rubbed my hands together. At last, the feeling of belonging which had eluded me began to fade.

•

"Who does homework on Saturday night?" I grumbled. Assuming that I must work harder than most others was downright frustrating! Finally, I had finished my book report on John Steinbeck's *The Red Pony*. I placed my typewriter back in its case and closed the lid. Having been taught to us in Halifax starting at age eleven, typing now proved to be a useful skill for handing in print assignments.

However, without braille materials at my fingertips, Mom became my talking textbook. "Could you repeat that, please?" Reading for myself would have been so much easier to retain information, but, Mr. Olivier had kept his word, "Don't expect any help from us, and I guarantee that we will not supply you with braille books."

Academic challenges could be overcome, but what I longed for, was acceptance among my peers. Unlike Katherine and Tamara, wearing cool clothes wasn't merely enough to boost my self-esteem. While their goal was to stand out, mine was to blend in. How was that even possible when I'm carrying that dreadful white cane? Poppycock! Listen to me. Now I'm as petty as other teenage girls and their tiresome fashion contests.

By April, I resigned myself that communication from other girls would go no further than, "Here I am, latch on," as they led me from class to class. Oh wait! There was that one day when they showed a spark of curiosity.

In mid spring, we students were huddled together on the school grounds. The air was downright nippy, evident by the stubborn snowbanks which refused to disappear. Ten minutes passed, and the fire alarm ceased its ear-splitting racket.

"When can we go back inside?" Katherine's teeth chattered.

"Yeah," Tamara complained, "the wind is blowing right through my blouse!"

Granted, I was shivering too, but I couldn't resist.

"This is nothing! You should try having a fire drill at 4 a.m."

"What?" the prissy pair gasped.

I laughed at their reaction. "Yep. It would happen to us at least once a year in Halifax."

"What was that like," Tamara asked.

For the first time, I felt like they had an interest in learning something about me.

"Scary! Kids on my floor helped each other down three flights of stairs, then we'd stand outside in our pyjamas. When it was over we'd go back to our rooms, but no one could fall asleep after something like that."

As I finished my story, Ms. Violett took one more head count. I held Tamara's arm, as we were given the all- clear to enter the building again.

•

In mid June, I pressed the play button on my cassette machine. I listened with anticipation to Kara's voice. After all, the exchange of letters on tape with my former roommate was the closest thing I had to a real friendship.

As she recited the latest school gossip, years of homesickness seemed oddly less significant. In Halifax there was always that camaraderie, as we lived together, played together, ate together, went to school together. Suddenly, Kara's voice extinguished these memories into cold reality.

"By the way," she continued, "I talked to Mr. Olivier last week, and told him that you were thinking about coming back in the fall."

Admittedly, I had conveyed to Kara that I may have no choice but to return to Halifax. After revealing these same concerns to Mom, I perceived disappointment in her reply, "You have to do what you feel is right for you."

Now hearing Mr. Olivier's response to Kara, my heart pounded. "Oh, I knew all along that she couldn't do it alone. Cheryl just wants someone to hold her hand."

I was stunned! I ripped my cassette tape from the recorder, and heaved it across the room. "Jerk!" I fumed. "It's all your fault! I hate you!"

I knew it! Mr. Olivier had deliberately withheld braille materials to undermine any success I may have in public school.

I stood up, collected myself, and made my way to the kitchen to talk to Mom. "I'll show him," I resolved. "I'm not going back!"

Chapter 13
BLACK AND GOLD

Established in 1785, FHS was the first English speaking high school in Canada. We had the largest student population in the British Commonwealth — approximately 3500 in my graduating year.

When I attended Fredericton High School, we had a fairly new building, a complex web of corridors which I soon learned to navigate. I contacted the CNIB and without delay, they willingly sent a mobility instructor to provide me with assistance.

•

It all started on shaky ground: I mean, the love-hate connection between me and the white cane. While in Halifax, the comment "Cheryl lacks motivation," as written by the mobility instructor on my final report-card wasn't quite an accurate assessment. I remember it well, how every dip and crack of the city's concrete blocks would jar my aching joints. Yes, he was most definitely aware of my arthritis, and no, this was never factored into our training sessions.

As I entered public school in Fredericton, my opposition to the white cane stemmed out of being seen as *different* from other kids. After all, its very imagery seemed to scream, "You are blind!" When learning of my concern, Bill Turney of the CNIB presented me with a new cane: the top having a black rubber grip, the middle portion being white and the bottom segment, red. Sure, it was still a cane, but for whatever reason it made me feel less conspicuous.

In time, I began to embrace everything from a new perspective. I was determined: this white cane was one mechanism toward my independence, a useful implement in which to "stick it" to Mr. Olivier. From here on, I would be the one to call the shot, not him!

•

Clutched in my right hand, I tapped the white cane along a suburban sidewalk. For the life of me, I couldn't imagine what I was doing on this residential street. My request was simple: I needed to locate my classrooms at the high school. However, Larry Bono, a mobility instructor with the CNIB, had other ideas.

In the first meeting, Larry had my father and I parade arm in arm, up and down the narrow stairway of our house between the main floor and the bedrooms. After four awkward demonstrations, Dad remarked, "I don't see how this exercise has any benefit for Cheryl."

This was followed up with Larry and I arriving at my family's home church. "Walk down the centre aisle and with your cane, take note of the pews." Begrudgingly, I did as he asked, but again, how was this helping to locate my classrooms?

Now, here we were on Cherry Avenue more than three miles from the high school. I was beginning to question this man's credentials.

"Your cane just struck a power pole," he declared. "I want you to touch it, and sniff it, so you'll know what it is next time."

"I'm not doing that!" I was indignant! "You aren't getting it, Larry. The objective is to go to the high school and learn to find my way around there."

When we finally entered FHS, Larry instructed, "The first thing I'd like you to recognize is the metal floor- grate, just inside the door." Yes, this was good. I could feel it under my feet, my cane scraping over its rough surface. Familiarizing me with the school entrance, Larry had me pace back and forth on this eight-foot metal strip. After the tenth run-through, I got huffy. "Okay, pretty sure I know about the grate. Can we find my classrooms now?"

"I think we've done enough for today," he replied.

I had lost all patience with Mr. Bozo! My mouth became dry, and suddenly I felt woozy. Was I going to pass out?

"Now look!" With a crack in my voice I sputtered, "There is less than a week before school starts, and I still don't know where my classes will be. You're wasting my time!"

•

At home, I picked up the phone to call Bill Turney. I really liked Bill. He had a knack for dealing with everyone, and especially with an outspoken, forthright teenager. After informing him that I had no further use for Larry Bono, I remember hearing his devilish giggle, and the pet name he had given me, "My little spitfire!"

"I'm serious," I reiterated, trying not to smile. "Don't bother sending him back! My father will help me instead."

•

At the school administration desk, Dad and I received a copy of my Grade 10 schedule. "Well...let's see," he pondered. "Looks like your first class is on the top floor."

Dad was surprisingly thorough. He determined which might be the quickest route to each class, whether by taking the stairs or by the elevator. He showed me to my locker, conveniently located across from a girls' washroom. Down a nearby hallway and four doors to the right, would be my homeroom class. If a room was opened, Dad would guide me to a desk closest to the door. If it was locked, he'd peer through the window and describe the layout to me.

After navigating the route with me several times he asked, "What do you think?"

"Can we do it once more?"

"I don't mind at all. We can do this as many times as you like."

I honestly didn't expect this level of patience from my father. He wouldn't stop until I was sure of myself, and at last, I felt ready.

•

On my first day at Fredericton High School, I timidly stepped off the bus, and once inside headed toward my locker. Okay, focus! Listening to my surroundings, I veered left to avoid a cluster of kids in the hallway. Did they not see me? As I approached the elevator, I heard a clanking of a mop and bucket. "Be careful, the floor is wet," the janitor cautioned. I thanked him as I entered the elevator, pressing the top button, each having an embossed print number beside it.

Yes! Dad had taught me well. I hung my jacket, and placed my paper-bagged lunch on the locker's bottom shelf. Fortunately, I had been granted permission to eat in the classroom, rather than face the noise and bustle of the school cafeteria. Turning the key, I secured my belongings and continued down the hall where I would locate my History class.

Although well intentioned, Mrs. Parker was too much of a mother hen for my liking. "Oh! Let me tie your shoes for you," she fussed.

"No, I'll do it," I replied firmly. Of course, she couldn't have known that I had left my laces loose on purpose, as it was easier on my joints to tighten them while seated at my desk. Indeed, I had started off on the wrong foot with Mrs. Parker, but there was something about her that irritated me.

First, there was the way she spoke to her Grade 10 students, as though we were kindergarten children, and perhaps more so to the blind girl in their midst. Then, when Mrs. Parker quite indiscreetly whispered answers to me prior to a test, my classmates justifiably voiced their disapproval. And who could blame them? It irked me! I didn't ask to be spoon-fed, and I didn't want to be singled out. Her incessant coddling was like a pesky mosquito you might want to swat!

During our study of Greek history, Mrs. Parker's assignment required us to write "An Ode to a Grecian Urn." Evidently, this exercise demanded we include a cutout of an urn for which to complement the poem.

Although I enjoyed writing, what was I to do about this visual aspect of our homework? Afterward, once students were dismissed I inquired, "Am I also expected to take a picture from out of a magazine?"

"Everyone is doing it — no exceptions." Mrs. Parker snipped. "Your mother will have to cut and glue it on the page for you."

How absurd! Days later, I informed Mom that, together, we had received a ten out of ten on our collaborative "arts and crafts" project!

•

In November, Mom made her one and only appearance at the FHS parent-teacher interviews. Things went well until she entered my biology classroom. My mother had barely introduced herself before the teacher blurted, "If you think I am going to give Cheryl any special treatment because she is blind, you are sorely mistaken!"

Mom was dumbstruck! "I'm not here to request favours — I simply came in support of my daughter. That's it!" Incensed by the woman's rude assumption, my mother turned and quickly walked away.

•

Gradually, braille books for math, French, biology, and even the periodic table of elements for my chemistry class began to trickle in. Oh! What satisfaction it was to envision Mr. Olivier waving a flag of surrender at my determination to remain in public school.

While in Grade 11, my fingers skimmed over the title of our history textbook. Just my luck! It was the same one we had studied in Grades Seven and Eight in Halifax. I was cursed! I hated it then, and I was certain it would be no different now.

Mr. Franklin's monotone delivery of European history did little to enhance my interest for the subject. Still, he deserved credit; whenever I asked, he was always there to provide extra help at lunchtime. Punctuated by his soup slurps and banana smacks, he'd calmly drill me on those mind-numbing wars, alliances and peace treaties.

•

By this time, I had adjusted to public school and my confidence grew. I no longer kept ties with anyone in Halifax, which is why on one particular day, I was completely thrown.

In math class, I was absorbed in algebra when interrupted by a knock at the door. "It's for you," my teacher revealed. After stepping into the hallway, I was greeted by someone from administration who informed me that my presence had been requested. After showing me to an office, the lady then guided my hand to a nearby chair. Why all the secrecy?

"Hello Cheryl," I heard a man's voice from across the room. "Do you know who this is?"

"No," I replied uneasily. I hated these types of guessing games.

"It's Mr. Moffat. Do you remember me?"

While in Halifax, Mr. Moffat was by far my favourite teacher. But what on earth was he doing here?

"It's been a long time, Cheryl. How are you?" "Good."

"I hear you're doing well in school." "Yup."

As though I were defending my territory, I mentally drew a line to protect my personal stomping-grounds from Mr. Moffat.

"Well, I'm in Fredericton for a conference, and I thought I would stop by to see how you're doing."

"Oh," I said guardedly. While fidgeting with my white cane, a stifled hush had fallen between us. I then heard myself utter, "Can I go now?"

"Sure," he answered, conveying a hint of disappointment. "All the best, Cheryl."

"Thanks," I muttered, nearly bumping into a wall as I bolted from the room.

It took a moment to get my bearings before heading back to class. On the way, my hands were dreadfully cold, much like the reception I had given Mr. Moffat. Was this really a friendly visit, or was he spying on me? Reflecting on his parting words, he did appear to be especially hurt. In time, I would recognize my deep-seeded fear — the lie which challenged me, saying 'maybe I'll be pressured to go away, again.' Such thoughts, regrettably, had influenced my lousy behaviour toward this man.

•

The single thing that would have made my life complete, was music. However, after three years of inquiries, nobody seemed interested in taking on a blind student. I had all but given up when one day, the phone rang. It was Bill Turney, informing my mother that a piano teacher had come forward!

I adored Mr. Davis! He was kind, patient, and his laughter was amusingly spirited. Each Thursday during my lunch period, he and I met at the high school, where I had lessons in the music department. Fortunately, I was also granted permission to practice there twice per week.

Given that I had been away from the piano for so long, Mr. Davis felt it best to start me from the beginner "Leila Fletcher" collection. Just as well, as by now I had forgotten some of the braille music code. "Find bars 5 and 13," he'd say, making comparisons between our print and braille copies. "What similarities do you see? Crescendos? Staccatos?" Although he was a non-braille reader, in this way, Mr. Davis helped to refresh my memory, enabling me to interpret most of the music symbols.

And there was more good news! Arriving home from school, I had carried an armful of braille books to my room when I heard Mom call out, "Cheryl! Can you come downstairs?"

"What! Did I forget something?"

"No," she said with an air of mystery. Yanking me toward the dining-room, Mom placed my hand on the piano keys.

"Look! You have your own piano!" The words practically danced from her lips.

I must be dreaming! Stroking its ivory keys, I heard bits of the story as Mom related how this all came to pass. Acquired from a retired music teacher in Perth, my parents, along with a few of my Gillespie aunts and uncles chipping in, had delivered it to me. It was a Willis upright grand, made in Montreal in 1919. And now, it was all mine!

•

As often said, 'your senior year in high school will be the best one' was definitely true for me. It took some convincing, but a sociology classmate eventually persuaded me to join the FHS Glee Club. As we were both in the soprano section, I was able to sit beside her in the choir. Everyone was good-natured and welcoming. I felt like I belonged. This led me to join two more music groups — the Girls' Chorus, and the Madrigal Singers — all under the direction of Tom Morrison.

Another highlight was participating in the musical, "West Side Story." For sure, I was a blond-haired Puerto

Rican! Nope, it didn't matter that I was merely a singing wall-flower as I was beyond thrilled to be a part of this large production. True, the months of weekend and after school rehearsals leading to our four shows were exhausting, but I loved every minute of it.

My last event was a school exchange program, wherein the FHS band and choirs all boarded a bus destined for Cornwall, Ontario. Energized by the adrenalin of our school musical, it was natural to think this trip would be another gratifying experience. Of course, our singing performances would be second to none, but I hadn't foreseen having to cope with those stow-away flashbacks which tagged along for the ride.

Perhaps it should have been a sign of things to come when, en route, we had stopped to eat in Quebec. As I recall, the diner episode was rather unpleasant as a number of students became ill due to food poisoning.

While in Cornwall, a Dutch family acted as hosts for me and two other girls from the FHS choir. Don't get me wrong — the people were lovely, and their hospitality generous. For me, however, subtle memories of Halifax seemed to lurk around every corner. Could it have been the unfamiliar surroundings — the foreign cuisine — or the thought of us three girls and the host's daughter all sharing a room? Whatever the case, I felt an overwhelming sense of déjà vu.

If that weren't enough, while at the closing dance I overheard my companions make a phone call to the Dutch parents to come and pick me up. Evidently, I was cramping their style!

The lady of the house apologized for the ill-mannered teens. "I'm fine," I insisted, fluffing my bed pillow with a little extra oomph. "You don't have to stay with me, I'd sooner be alone."

Once she had left the room, I couldn't hold back the tears. Fumbling for my suitcase, I made sure everything was packed since we would be getting an early start in the morning. Drained from the entire journey, I was relieved when our bus pulled up to the school in Fredericton once again.

•

Overall, I loved my senior year. I possessed braille books, I was involved in all things music, and I had adapted well to life in high school. I didn't want it to end. Besides, what would my future be like after graduation?

In late spring, the Grade 12 students were required to answer a vast number of questions on a test called "Choices" sponsored by Canada Manpower. Read to me over a span of two days, I responded to each one to the best of my ability. It consisted of a random selection such as:

Which of the following are you more inclined to do? Circle one.

A: Feed barnyard chickens.
B: Read to the blind.
C: Paint a house.

Once completed, our data was entered into a computer and students would learn which occupation they were most recommended to explore. Three weeks passed. Mom and I had fixed our hopes on its outcome in order to give me a clear direction. The day it came in the mail, my mother ripped the envelope open, and read the results to herself.

"What!" I waited impatiently.

I wasn't inspired by her tone. "Well," she paused… "It says that you should pursue a career as an airline pilot."

I was speechless! Had my employment prospects been dispensed from a gumball machine? Mom broke our silence.

"Oh come on," she joked, "you'd be an excellent pilot, don't you think?"

"Yeah, sure! I can see it now. 'Welcome to *White Cane Airlines*.'"

"Don't worry," my mother encouraged. "One day, you'll know what it is you want to do."

•

I can't recall why, but my class of 850 grad students voted against the traditional cap and gown attire. On graduation night, my pretty white dress, dotted with mauve flowers, matched the dainty corsage around my wrist. Students were permitted to invite four guests, and it was Mom, Dad, Thomas and my grandmother Goodine who were seated in the stands of the Aitken University Centre.

Although the ice surface was covered by a layer of carpet, a chill had seeped through and my feet quickly became numbed. Now, at the conclusion of numerous speeches, it was time to announce the hundreds of graduate names. As I was led to the stage, the arena exploded in applause! Presented to me was the scroll-like diploma, wrapped with ribbons in our school colours of black and gold. Inside, a seal that read:

Palma Non Sine Pulvere, translation, *"No Reward Without Effort."*

Chapter 14

ME AND OLD WILLIS

With graduation behind me, I faced the stark reality of "What will I do now?" The self-assurance I had gained during my final year of public school had been rudely snatched from my fingers and I was unprepared for making my own way in the world. Nevertheless, immediately after high school I was offered a summer position with the CNIB. Teamed up with a university student hired to give dictation, my task was to transcribe, into braille, articles like restaurant menus, city transit schedules, or official government directories. How gratifying it was to earn a paycheque, but why was I so miserable?

At the end of each workday, I'd retreat to my bedroom, change my clothes and curl up under a blanket. Throughout the week, my conversations with family members were brusk. "Yup! Nope! Don't know! Doesn't matter!" Occasionally, I'd hear myself making curt remarks
— as with interruptions, "Is this Grand Central? ... Can't you see I'm practicing piano?" Or when at meal-time, "We're having this, again?"

Piecing it all together, Mom approached me one Sunday afternoon. "You know," she paused, being careful to choose her words, "I've noticed by the end of the weekend, your mood is far better. I'm curious, is there air conditioning in your office?"

"Yeah," I replied, wondering where this was leading.

"I think the cold air is affecting your joints. You may not realize it, but when your arthritis acts up, it shows, and you are hard to live with."

Not only had Mom called out my moodiness, but she had identified my physical suffering. Why was this a revelation to me? The truth is, I've since learned that when one develops a tolerance for pain, it is often indiscernible. If I'm not careful, it may very well manifest itself in unkind words.

COPING LESSON NUMBER 1: Be mindful of my demeanour when pain is buried beneath the surface.

•

Perhaps I thought it was expected of me: in September, I enrolled at the University of New Brunswick. Again, there were no braille textbooks, nor had I received counsel for which direction I might strive toward in my post secondary education. Without a single goal, I considered, *was this really the right path for me?*

As I arrived on campus, I stepped off a passenger-crammed bus and exhaled its heavy vinyl odour from my lungs. "Get your bearings," I told myself. Relying on my spatial senses and my white cane, I zigzagged around a few parked cars before reaching a flight of stairs. Once inside, more obstacles awaited. I inched through a group of loitering students, then collided into sporadically placed armchairs and ashtrays before being rescued by my professor of child psychology.

When I had effectively located my last course of the day, this one in music rudiments, Professor Freddezza met me at the door.

"Oh," he said, preventing my entrance to the room, "you're attending this class?"

"Yes," I beamed, as this was the one subject which appealed to me.

"I'm not sure this is the class for you." I was confused. "Why is that?"

Evidently Professor Freddezza had heard something of my background as he queried, "Haven't you already covered the technique of scales and triads?"

"Well, yes — I completed my RCM exam in June, with an 84%."

"Very good," he went on, "and you know your key signatures and time values, correct?"

Pleased with myself, I again answered, "Yes."

"You don't belong here. I'm afraid you'd be bored since you already know the topics which are outlined in this course."

Professor Freddezza then wished me well, closed the door, and there I stood in the hallway, alone.

At first, I was flattered by his suggestion that, somehow, this material was beneath me. He aimed to persuade me that I was ahead of the others when, in fact, I had barely scratched the surface of music theory. The more I thought about it, the more I realized how tense he appeared in my presence. It was obvious... Professor Freddezza did not want me in his class!

By late October, I skipped one day, then another. However brief, there was absolutely nothing stimulating about my experience at UNB. Granted, I had received an A-plus on the child psychology report written merely from mental notes (there were no braille materials available). Thereafter, I informed Mom that I would be dropping out of my university courses.

•

Each morning, I awakened to our empty home — my parents at their respective jobs and my siblings in school. Seldom one to twiddle my thumbs, I engaged in a routine of household chores: washing dishes, making beds, vacuuming, or laundering what seemed an ever-growing mountain of towels. It was therapeutic. I knew I should remain productive and, while doing so, I learned how much Mom had appreciated the extra help.

Cooking was indeed my mother's area of expertise. Although she taught me useful tips on baking desserts and preparing my favourite foods, for some reason, the day came when she underestimated her own advice.

"Cheryl, it wouldn't hurt to call the CNIB to see if they have special cooking instructions for the blind."

"No way!"

"Please," she urged, "will you do this? They may have a few methods unknown to me."

The CNIB lady was pleasant, yet apologetic. Her culinary technique 101 assignment was as follows:

"Pour packaged cake mix into bowl, add water and stir." Clearly, I would be no threat to the world of gourmet chefs!

•

More than anything, it was me and my Willis upright grand which defined my days with a sense of purpose. The practice of music had never been an arduous process for me — rather, it was rewarding for my body and soul, an escape from all my insecurities.

Still, I often wished I were back in high school — surrounded by friends, sharing music with them — while at the same time I believed there must be further prospects for me in this world. Why wasn't I tuned in? Why hadn't I figured it out?

Sliding the piano bench into place, I turned toward the beckoning sunshine. "Aren't you the smart one," I praised Miss Kitty, offering her a light head-scratch. She had flopped on a warm stretch of carpet, just in front of the patio glass door... oh, to have the untroubled life of a cat!

Alas, there were things I knew for certain — I did not enjoy this empty phase of my life, nor did I like the awful feeling of loss. And yet...it was happening, again. Since graduation, my piano teacher Mr. Davis had remained a constant for me, that is, until the day he revealed the upsetting news: we would have only three more sessions before his transfer to Hamilton, Ontario.

•

During our final lesson in Christ Church Cathedral Hall, I forced a smile at his goofy humour, yet deep down, I was trying to hold it together. I remembered the day when Mr. Davis had convinced me to perform a duet with him at an upcoming recital. He knew me so well — this was the perfect way to introduce me to playing in public. It's ironic when I think of it — our piece was the theme from "The Exodus." After working with Mr. Davis for only two years, it now hit me: this would be the last time I'd play my grade seven pieces for him before he left the province.

Having called a cab, Mr. Davis and I walked side by side toward the main door. Just then, a man, who had shuffled in from behind us, required his attention. Momentarily, my taxi had also arrived. I turned around to face Mr. Davis and his chatty stranger. Should I wait for him? No! I just couldn't — and without saying goodbye I slipped out, weeping the whole drive home.

•

Meanwhile, Mr. Davis had prearranged for me to study with a new teacher in town, Mrs. Bradshaw. No doubt, this woman was eccentric! Flaunting a sophisticated accent, she delighted in telling stories of her trips abroad, of her repulsive appetite for snake soup and those grandiose depictions of her piano concerts.

Whereas I had been formerly trained by constructive disciplines, I somehow managed to stick it out under Mrs. Bradshaw's teaching style for nearly five months. With that in mind, as I'd finish playing, she was more apt to gush some meaningless fluff, like, "Simply exquisite," then sniff and pull out a tissue to blow her nose.

At the conclusion of one such colourful meeting, she announced, "By the way, a recital will take place on Saturday and I would like you to perform your Bach prelude." Caught off guard, I wrestled with the zipper of my winter coat, imploring, "I'm not comfortable playing in front of people."

"Oh, but you must! All of my students will perform, otherwise they will not study with me."

By this time, my mother was due to arrive. Mrs. Bradshaw and I had reached an impasse, and I did not think much of her ultimatum. "Fine by me!" I slammed the door in protest, no longer to return.

•

Weeks later, Mrs. Bradshaw showed up at my house. "I am truly sorry, Cheryl. I shouldn't have put you in that position. Can you forgive me?"

"Yes," I mumbled, suspicious that she had another agenda in mind.

"Darling, listen! I have a fabulous idea! I'd like you to consider giving piano lessons. There are two children in my neighbourhood whom I can recommend, as I am unable to take them myself."

She couldn't be serious!

"How can I teach sighted kids? I don't know what print music looks like, and I..."

"Rubbish!" Mrs. Bradshaw cut in. Grabbing my hand, she began to draw squiggly shapes into my palm. "See? This is a quarter note."

Although I had reservations, I agreed to take a chance on teaching music, despite her last admonishment.

"One more thing. If a student asks you a question for which you have no answer, never admit that you do not know."

•

I soon discovered that conducting piano lessons from my family's home was less than ideal. The TV could be heard from the basement or the phone would ring, and in typical teenaged fashion, my sisters casually sashayed into the room, glancing in the mirror before heading out to join their friends. Was it really necessary to primp themselves in this very spot, or were they just nosy?

As expected, I jumped into my new career having no clue what I was doing. Thankfully, the kids gave excellent descriptions of what was on the printed page and I did my best to interpret it for them. At the very least, finger numbers beside music notes provided a means for which my beginner students might follow along — but let's be honest, I was a terrible teacher!

On the other hand, Mrs. Bradshaw's — although weirdly wacky — encouragement, together with my first exposure to teaching piano students, had initiated a thought process of what my future might look like. Gradually, I purchased a set of table and chairs, kitchenware, and linens. I also obtained a braille book aimed toward early music educators, versing myself on its respective methodologies.

"You can do it," I declared aloud, poising myself for what would be, to me and old Willis — the big move!

Chapter 15
IMPERFECT HARMONY

The aged house on Main Street was divided into three apartments, one upstairs, one downstairs, and mine at ground-floor level. I had a larger than average-sized bathroom and, in the bedroom, an abundance of storage with built-in units consisting of twelve drawers and two closets. There was a farm-style kitchen, complete with lots of cupboards, a china cabinet and a U-shaped countertop. Just off the kitchen was a little nook which became the home for my old Willis.

Even with an ad in the newspaper and flyers for piano lessons distributed throughout our neighbourhood, I worried. What if I couldn't enrol enough students? How would I support myself? My fears were alleviated as the phone rang off the hook and in no time, I had twenty-four students! What's more, my mother offered $100 for three consecutive months. I could now breathe easier — I was financially secure and ready to stand on my own two feet.

•

My expectations were realistic. I had no illusions of existing in a dulcet world; then again, I hadn't quite braced myself to encounter a dimwitted public.

It started before moving to Main Street, when I was met with resistance from potential landlords, the 'not under my roof syndrome.' Somehow, these closed-minded people assumed I was gullible enough to believe they were concerned for my safety.

"Oh, no dear! We can't have you living here as there are stairs, and you might fall."

Hmph! I've been walking up and down stairs all my
life.

"Well," came another flimsy argument, "we're afraid you may burn yourself on our stove."

Aww! Their regard for my well-being was touching! Sceptical, I mused that they must be protecting themselves from pending lawsuits.

"Yes dear," a woman indulged, "you can stay, as long as you have a roommate to look after you."

"I don't need a babysitter."

"Of course not," she clarified her position. "My issue is... you might flood the toilet and not realize it for days."

Of all the inane statements! Fingers tightened on the phone, I mustered my composure. "For your information, I do understand the concept of wet!" When hanging up, I emphatically gave the telephone receiver a satisfactory bang! Although I later discovered that toilet lady and I attended the same church, my inclination was to contact people I did not know. My reasons: I hated the idea that someone in my circle might feel obliged; or worse, take pity on me... But now, what choice did I have?

At the time, my hairdresser had acquired a house wherein she rented three apartments and set up her shop. "Hello... no... I don't need an appointment. I was wondering...do you have any apartments available?" Struggling to control the quaver in my voice, I related my recent encounters. I can't say for certain if she felt sorry for me, or if she would have offered her accommodations anyway. The bottom line is she did, and thus began my life of independence.

•

Groceries were an easy proposition. Just as my mother had done in her early days, I too picked up the phone to place an order. The store clerks were excellent, and on only two occasions do I recall raising eyebrows at items in the delivery. "What is this," I uttered aloud, examining a large, shelled coconut, instead of the shredded kind I had requested for baking a dessert. Or the second time, when I poured from a newly opened carton and heard a *plop, plop,* of curdled milk in my glass.

Invariably, my belongings were tidy and all surfaces dust free. For the most part, unless I became ill, my home was spotless, something in which I took great pride. Therefore, after a student's parent had asked, "Who does your cleaning for you," I had to refrain from pointed remarks like, "Seriously! As if I could afford a housekeeper!"

•

With only a few weeks to prepare for two dozen students, Bill Turney of the CNIB invited me to meet an individual in the province who could offer guidance. I accepted, as I would need all the help I could get.

John Ramsay was a respected musician, teacher, and piano tuner in the Miramichi region. Although his knowledge and experience were far beyond what I would ever accomplish, I immediately sensed an impish spirit about him.

Sitting in a small den, the three of us became acquainted. The air was stuffy, as though windows had not been opened all summer. Nevertheless, an unsettling chill came over me when John asked, "I understand you also attended the school in Halifax, Cheryl?"

"Yes," I bristled, "some time ago." I rubbed away the goosebumps from my arms as if to erase those prickly thoughts from my memory.

"Oh, what great times I had there!"

My ears perked up. "Really?" It hadn't occurred to me that perhaps not everyone shared my sentiment of the school for the blind.

"Why yes!" he reminisced. "I was there in the 1930s, long before you." He chuckled, and proceeded to entertain us with his personal anecdotes.

"As I recall," he began, "there was one occasion when we hosted two board members who had travelled from a blind school in England. Not sure why, but I was assigned the duty of leading these gentlemen on a tour of our building."

"When you walk, do you count your steps?" one guest queried.

"I used to do that," I spoke mischievously, "but one day I bought a pair of shoes that were an inch longer than my old ones. Thereafter, I kept over-shooting the mark and bumping into walls!"

"Ah! We have a cheeky lad!"

Curiously, the absurd interview continued. "Do blind people feel colours?"

"No, not all colours" I baited the Englishman. "What do you mean?"

"Well, sometimes I feel blue!"

I laughed, appreciating the comic relief of John's stories. Maybe we had a connection, after all. My mood considerably lighter, he then encouraged me in my music aspirations.

"You are a smart girl, Cheryl. Teaching music is a worthy pursuit. Of course, there's much to learn, but you have your whole life ahead of you. And remember, I am here whenever you need to chat."

Before leaving his home, John sent me away with an armful of braille piano books, an invaluable gesture to start my career. He wished me well, and Bill Turney and I continued on our two-hour trip to Fredericton.

•

John Ramsay was right. I had much to learn, and thus, I continued with my music studies. Again, Bill was instrumental in locating a teacher on my behalf, this time, for vocal lessons.

I looked forward to the many hours when Mrs. Schemmée would train me in those beautiful French, Italian, and German art songs. For me, singing had always offered an emotional release whether in my dorm in Halifax, or after joining the choirs either in high school or at my church.

"You're a lyric soprano," she informed me, and in a short time my voice soared beyond what I had ever imagined.

During one of our sessions, I described a barrier I faced in properly instructing kids to read music notes. I told her about Mrs. Bradshaw's hasty doodles in the palm of my hand, and the poor counsel to never admit to a student the things you do not know.

"That is the worst advice I have ever heard!" She scoffed in disbelief. "As for your dilemma, leave it with me. It's important for you to have an understanding of print music and I will help you with it."

One day, Mrs. Schemmée stopped by, overjoyed to show me what she had designed. An old chalkboard was now layered with felt material, and on it, Velcro strips which represented the lines of the music staff. Attached beneath the board was more fabric sewn into four pockets. In each of these slots were cut-out shapes of quarter, half, and whole notes, the treble and bass clef, along with a variety of other music symbols.

What an inspiration! After she had taken her time to demonstrate how these signs are placed on the staff, Mrs. Schemmée, equipped with hooks and hammer, hung my new music board on the wall of my little piano nook.

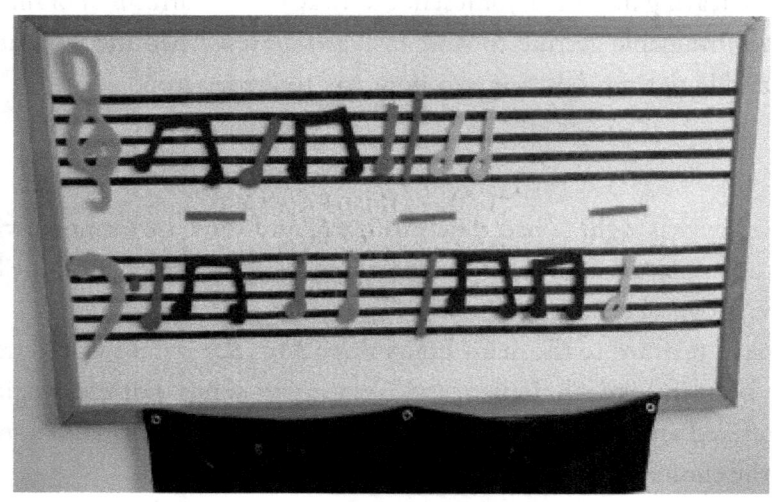

"There!" she exclaimed. "It's my gift to you. From now on, you'll have the tactile tools to be the teacher I know you can be."

•

As well as voice lessons, I determined to further my education in piano, theory, history and harmony. These music credits would be attained through the Royal Conservatory under the private direction of Mr. Hanson. His analytical mind, his uncanny perceptiveness, were the precise qualities I needed in a mentor.

Recitals... master classes? My tendency would have been to shy away from such things were it not for this man. A heart to heart conversation and a subtle suggestion later, I would find myself performing in front of an audience or playing for a professor of music from Acadia University.

Finally! The study of this history course was one in which I could identify! Music, it would appear, was the missing key necessary to open the pages of the past, of ancient rulers, evolving civilizations, of period architecture and literature. With all this, a braille book three editions behind the print world made it achievable, and yet, having no materials for harmony was a major inconvenience.

What fresh purgatory was this! Looking back, we reasoned that there must have been a degree of madness to endure those late-night phone calling, hair-pulling, music dictating sessions. At the outset, Mr. Hanson and I didn't quite speak the same language, as he thought of music in vertical terms and I in horizontal. With that resolved, I completed my first harmony assignment. "Congratulations!" he expressed in familiar dry humour. "You have successfully composed a Gregorian chant!" Oof! Not especially pleasing to my ears, but forging ahead, each successive step would ultimately contribute toward my growth as a competent musician and teacher.

•

Admittedly, I would have doubted my abilities to teach at all, were it not for those few students who demonstrated an aptitude toward music. On my side, however, was the desire to succeed, but as I soon discovered, my calling required more than music education. It was also about featuring each child's unique gifts, and to my dismay, addressing occasional misbehaviours.

Such matters weren't merely of pulling the wool over the blind teacher's eyes. It was more about my inexperience, as was the case with one naughty little girl.

Cupped between her hands, Molly jingled a few coins. "Guess what I have," the seven-year-old chattered.

"Sounds like money to me."

"Yep, I found it on the playground at school." "Aren't you lucky! How about you put it in your pocket during our lesson."

Instead, the girl spread her new found treasure on my kitchen table. Following our session, I reminded Molly to gather up her loose change but after two weeks of prompting, she had deliberately left it behind. What kid doesn't want to possess a handful of money?

At the earliest opportunity, I turned the coins over to her mother. "I believe she took it from our dresser," the woman revealed. "Molly knows she's not allowed to do that."

Her second stunt was a cause for more bewilderment. As our lesson finished, Molly spotted homemade muffins which I had set to cool on the kitchen counter.

"Mmm! I love muffins! Can I have one?"

Why not, I thought. A nice snack for her walk on the way home.

The next week, Molly and her mother arrived together. The girl pranced into the kitchen, singing at the top of her lungs.

"I'm sorry," her mother said, appearing flustered. "I should inform you that I will be driving Molly to her lessons from now on."

"Oh?"

"You see," she explained, "when Molly got home last week, she told her father and I that a woman tried to kidnap her. We immediately called the police. In amazing detail, she described to the officer all about the woman who slowed her car, opened the window and offered a muffin to lure her inside. Molly declined — but somehow, she was able to get the license plate number and run home as fast as she could."

I was speechless! The whole story sounded fishy. If I exposed the girl, she would be in a heap of trouble. And... what if the mother didn't believe me?

"Did the police find anyone?"

"They traced the license plate and questioned someone who lives on a nearby street. The officer concluded the person had nothing to do with the incident. Who knows, perhaps Molly was off by a digit or two, poor thing! Listen to her... she is humming away like nothing happened!"

My stomach sank. I couldn't say anything to this doting mother. Chances were she'd trust her little angel.

Once alone with the child, I declared, "Time for our lesson, Molly."

"La, la, la!" Her song had now become irritating! "Well well! That must have been quite a scare. Do you remember when I gave you a muffin to take on your walk home?"

Molly grabbed her piano book and plunked herself on the bench. "Okay, I'm ready to play now," she said, refusing to acknowledge my question. From that time forward, I was very leery of Miss Molly muffin.

•

Years passed, and I grew wise. I mustn't be naive, as kids will be kids, and when the opportunity presents itself, some will take advantage of the situation at hand. Their mistake, however, is underestimating my superb hearing.

First up — the distracted boy. A crinkly page-turn confirmed my suspicion. This didn't sound at all like his music book.

"What are you reading?"

"Um... ah," he stammered. "It's my karate magazine."

Then there was the rambunctious girl who used my piano bench as a monkey bar, "Come on! Sit up, please!" "How did you know I was upside down?" she gasped. "That's not hard to figure when your head is speaking from the floor."

And years later, on one other occasion, following a barrage of thumb clicks from a fifteen-year-old, I warned, "I can hear that... put the phone away." If only this student had possessed the same dexterity on piano as was demonstrated in her texting.

•

More profound is the awe and acceptance shown to me by children which make them a delight to be around. Their curiosity is endearing, and the questions — priceless!

"Do I have to read that '*brayddle?*'" a five-year-old asked, trailing her fingers across a page of my book.

"Oh, no," I assured her. "Those dots are called braille, and it's my special way to read."

As we neared the end of a lesson, I pressed the button to check the time. "It's 3:57 p.m.," announced an unmistakably male voice.

"Is there a man in there?" the little girl giggled.

I smiled at her innocence. "No, it's just my talking clock."

"Do it again," she urged. "It's 3:58 p.m."

"How did he get in there? Can he hear us?"

•

I've come to realize, children are deep thinkers, too. They will ask, "When you dream can you see?" The quick answer to that is — no. In my dreams, I am still blind just as I am while I'm awake, but I'm able to perceive things around me.

I describe the phenomenon in this way. "Imagine seeing shapes or colours on a foggy day. You know, like watching TV, but with a snowy reception."

Of course, there is the inevitable, "What is it like to be blind? Is everything dark?"

"Pretend your eye is in your elbow," I aim to illustrate. "Do you see light? Shadows? Colours?" As they respond no to each question, I follow up with, "So, what do you see?"

"Nothing!"

"Exactly! And there's your answer."

•

Although I welcome questions from young and old alike, it never ceases to amaze me how tactless adults can be. In one instance, I met a Mennonite man who blurted, "How long have you been in the dark house?" I may not have been so red-faced if he hadn't humiliated me in front of others — each being rendered suddenly mute. Sensing all eyes on me and with only the tick-tock of a clock to break the silence, I fumbled for words, saying, "Blindness is not darkness." And with that, I recited to him the precise elbow analogy I've used with children.

By the same token, when out with a friend or family member, society has shown another type of ignorance by speaking to me in the third person. A bank clerk may ask, "Can she sign this?" while a hospital receptionist inquires, "Does she have her Medicare card?"

Bizarre! Evidently, my answers must vanish into oblivion, as people continue to direct their communication toward those who accompany me.

•

Whenever possible, however, I'd rely on my own mobility skills. On this particular day, a cab driver dropped me off at the door of the hospital. As I walked through what had become for me well-known territory, proceeding to my appointment, a man stopped to ask, "Would you like a wheelchair?"

"I'm fine," I replied, attempting to veer around him.

"It's no problem," he insisted, "I can get one for you."

I suppose the stranger had good intentions. I, on the other hand, was befuddled! How would he presume I maneuver a wheelchair while holding a white cane?

The YMCA was another regular commute that I'd travel without assistance. Swimming and aqua-fit, both low impact on my joints, were excellent ways to keep physically active. Albeit, on two separate occasions, it seemed the exercise was that of biting my tongue as I tried not to spew unfavourable sarcasm.

"You know, I'm going blind," I overheard a woman revealed to anyone who would listen. "It's awful! I can't cook. I can't clean. I can't do anything for myself!"

Having changed into my dry clothes, I shut the locker door. Should I empathize with her? After all, I've been blind my whole life and have learned to adapt. The woman then collected her white cane along with a set of car keys.

"Can I drive you home, Cheryl?"

After summoning a pity-party the woman was now getting behind the wheel — she and her white cane?

"No thanks!" I was disgusted! "I'll call a taxi."

On a rainy day, once again I entered the YMCA lobby. As usual, old Berny was talking to the girls at the front desk. He spotted me as I made my way through the crowd.

"That poor girl," he bellowed. "You know, she's blind! She comes to the Y because she has nothing to do all day long and is slowly going paralyzed!"

If only he had heard the wheel of insults churning within my mind — of all the blockheaded, cockamamie, obtuse assertions! Ugh! Who does he think he is? Little did he know, along with the YMCA, I was heavily involved at my church, taught 24 kids, and spent hours daily in study and practice of music. Why shouldn't I have been offended by this man's rhetoric?

•

Despite my efforts, however, I wished that I could do more. It was never blindness that repressed my ambitions; rather, my constant nemesis was fatigue. As my rheumatologist explained, "Sleep disorder is a consequential aspect of this chronic disease."

COPING LESSON NUMBER 2: Recognize what you cannot control, and work within its limitations.

It's not as though I had options... you deal with it. There were nights it seemed rest was overly exorbitant, and stretches of time when I'd experience sleep deprivation. All the same, I had a life with purpose. In time, I would come to terms with the weariness, and as always, observe a routine management of the pain from arthritis.

Chapter 16
MY CARES, MY PRAYERS

"Great news," announced my paediatrician.

"Fredericton finally has a rheumatologist!"

My stomach bunched into objectionable knots as memories returned to that child taunting, pretty-boy flaunting Dr. Peacock. My mind was set. By association, I had already determined not to like the new guy in town.

As I was not yet seventeen at the time of his debut, my parents made sure I would meet Dr. Henderson. Once out on my own, I felt I had no need for his expertise and skipped one or two appointments. Eventually, when I forced myself to make an appearance I discovered the doctor-patient dynamic had changed.

"We have to talk," he spoke firmly. "If I'm to be your rheumatologist, there has to be an understanding between us. I give you my word — the ultimate say on any treatment we discuss, will be yours. In return, I expect no more no-shows. Do we have a deal?"

I wasn't used to such candour. At last, I was empowered to make decisions concerning my own health, and from that moment onward, Dr. Henderson and I developed a mutual respect for each other.

It was January 3, when across the desk from me, I listened to an elaborate jotting of hasty scribbles and a couple of emphatic dots. The room fell quiet, as Dr. Henderson lay his pen down.

"Let's talk about this."

Oh-oh! This wasn't a good sign.

"I think we'd better admit you to hospital today." "What!" My mind raced. I had to go home and pack.

I needed to inform my students that lessons would be postponed.

"Please, can we do this tomorrow, instead?" "Alright," he consented. "But no later than 10 a.m."

•

In the morning, it was Thom who drove me to the hospital. How sweet of him to be the responsible, younger brother. He placed a few of my personal items inside the nightstand and made certain I was settled. "Mom will visit you after work," he assured me with a hug. "If you need anything, let me know and I can always drop it by. See you later."

Once Thom left, I lay back, pulled up a thin, cotton blanket and closed my eyes. During the past month, I had been sleeping about eighteen hours per day. I'd awake long enough to teach, nibble on a cracker or two, then fall into bed. To my dismay, I soon learned that a hospital is categorically no place in which to rest.

I recall when a parent of one of my students came to visit. She stayed for three hours, chatting and reading to me from magazine articles. She did the same the next day, and the day after that. How do you tell someone that their well- meaning deed is exhausting? Relieved, a nurse resolved my sticky situation. On her fifth social call, I heard a discussion outside my door about the "*Do Not Disturb*" sign.

"I'm sorry," she informed my frequent guest, "we are only permitting her family at this time."

What a small world — that night on evening shift entered another nurse, whose daughter had been a former student of mine. Initiating a polite exchange, she boasted to my elderly roommate in reference to my piano teaching. Inevitably, when the senior offered her own presumptive twist on the conversation to numerous visitors, I would have difficulty holding my tongue.

"That girl must be smart," the woman voiced in a meddlesome whisper. "She plays the piano. But those kinds of people are supposed to be musical, aren't they?" This was generally followed up with, "I'm sure she collects a blind pension. How else could she support herself?"

I had heard enough!

"Listen lady! I'm in the next bed. I can hear everything you say. You obviously have no sweet clue what you're talking about, so keep it to yourself!"

Believe me, I showed a fair bit of restraint given what I really wanted to say, "Look you old bat! My finances are none of your business. And… for your information, many blind people are about as musical as a dentist's drill!"

●

Along with sleep issues, pain and inflammation raged in nearly every joint. In the past month I had convinced myself — things would improve over the holidays.

Just eleven days prior my family and I all gathered around the table. How I had looked forward to Mom's home-cooking, to enjoying our traditional Christmas dinner. With a fork in my left hand, I merely picked away at the turkey. It was awkward. My right hand was too swollen to hold anything, and my jaw only partially opened. I ate very little, passed on her mincemeat pie — my seasonal favourite — and went straight to bed.

Living with a chronic disease, wellness has more to do with a vigilance of self-care rather than achieving complete remission. I had faired pretty well, though, due to the 'gold treatment' injections which had begun in Halifax a decade earlier. In my view, this was the only positive measure Dr. Peacock had taken in order to control my arthritis. As a twelve-year-old, I remember thinking I would become 'one big hole' having been jabbed with a needle every two weeks. Now, in my twenties, after an increase of weekly administrations of this drug, my immune system was no longer responding.

I was overwhelmed by the team of health professionals who worked diligently to get my life back on track. It began with technicians applying laser treatments as well as therapeutic ultrasound to alleviate joint inflammation. As the goose egg on my right wrist had been slow to shrink, Dr. Henderson suggested a cortisone injection to speed the process. True to his word, however, I would be the one who made the final decision — to continue on course with the laser treatment.

Amongst this medical group, the psychologist had especially ingrained on me words of lasting impact. We discussed the unpredictability of the disease, the limitations, and sometimes, the loneliness.

"On bad arthritis days, what reactions do you receive from your friends?"

At this point, I recognized most of my peers were those from church. Suddenly, her question reopened concealed thoughts which I had allowed to smoulder beneath the surface.

I was reminded of one instance when I made arrangements to go shopping, as a girl had earlier agreed she'd accompany me to the mall. "Can we try next weekend?" I spoke by phone, explaining to her that my joints were stiff and sore that day.

The response: "I think you're making an excuse!"

You bet it bothered me! Why should I have to defend my health to anyone?

Then there was that male acquaintance who tagged along with Mom and I to my brother's basketball tournament. As the game finished, my joints had stiffened and I struggled to walk.

"Come on," he said, pulling as I hobbled behind him, "it can't be that bad."

He backed off when Mom scolded, "Can't you see her limp? She isn't faking it."

COPING LESSON NUMBER 3: Where there is no acceptance, there is no real friendship.

•

After 24 days spent in hospital, I was ecstatic to go home. Upon my return, Joan, my youngest sister, had purchased a microwave oven to make cooking easier. As well, an occupational therapist had recommended ways to simplify day to day living. Until I had gained my strength, the therapist advised sitting on a kitchen stool to wash dishes. She also made a splint to support my wrist until fully recovered. Although beneficial, this device was not entirely functional — specifically when practicing for my upcoming piano exam.

•

Within four months and countless hours of rehearsal, I was ready! In contrast, I had not expected the examiner to be quite so unpolished.

On the stage of Christ Church Cathedral Hall, an RCM facilitator led me up to the grand piano. I then heard the examiner summon my guide in earnest, "Aren't you going to sit on the bench with her?"

"No!" I interrupted, taking great exception to this erroneous request. "It's my exam. I prepared for it, and I will be the only one sitting for it."

•

I hope I never become one of those crotchety old ladies who detail every toe stub and hangnail. However wearing it may be, I feel compelled to draw attention to two specific occurrences in my medical history.

First of all, there is nothing quite like a rock in one's head to cause persistent pain. Glaucoma had taken its toll, and my left eye had calcified. The evisceration was described as being similar to cutting into an orange skin, scooping out the contents, then filling it with a silicone ball before stitching it up. My eye would remain attached to muscle and tear ducts, so that when a prosthesis was fitted, it would move and appear as natural as possible.

Secondly, after having several arthroscopic surgeries, it had become necessary for me to undergo a right knee replacement. This was one instance where the idiom 'ignorance is bliss' would have suited me just fine. However, a music colleague who had experience in this regard, recounted the sights and sounds of hammers and saws used during the operation. I could have done without this carpentry visual, a depiction which scared me half to death!

Despite my fears, the surgery went exceptionally well. The physiotherapy was a tedious process, although worthwhile in order to rebuild muscles and to flex and straighten my new (titanium) knee. For sure, it hurt — but not like my childhood memories at the IWK hospital wherein the motto was "No Pain, No Gain." In my youth, the physical intensity subjected to my joints would cause certain harm — a tactic which is no longer encouraged these days.

•

For me, recovery is not solely derived through medicine. A large portion of it is attributed to my faith in God and by the healing effects of music.

It was a Sunday morning. As I waited for the Fraser family to drive me to church, I took my place at the piano, improvising on a few hymns. Hearing the robin outside my window, I was intrigued. When I played, he chirped. When I stopped, he hushed. As I picked up where I left off, once again he'd sing along. Remarkable! Evidently, God's creation also enjoys a pleasing melody.

Mr. and Mrs. Fraser were a lovely couple, and abundantly good to me. We shared telephone conversations, dawdling strolls on the church grounds, and occasional brunches at their house. Is there any doubt why most of the people I've trusted are of the older generation? I daresay it's because they've endured pain in life, whereas my younger counterparts had little understanding in this respect.

I had made one other friend at church — or so I thought. The day I heard she'd be attending Bible school in the fall, I expressed genuine happiness for her. Jokingly though, I blabbered aloud to her, "Oh, you can't go! Who will I have to talk to?"

"Get thee behind me, Satan!" came her sharp blow to my silly drama. She must have noticed the alarm on my face when she quickly apologized. Somewhat leery that I may be further burned, I distanced myself from her along with the rest of my age group — an action that didn't seem to faze them one way or the other. That said, it's not my wish to convey the wrong impression, as I did appreciate the amiability of my peers. It is just that I never got close enough to call them... friends.

One special memory, however, is that of our youth choir and the tour around New Brunswick and Prince Edward Island. With a tight schedule we would sing at a morning service, then travel to another church to perform that evening. Whenever we'd arrive early, about 2 PM, our music director instructed everyone to nap on pews — girls on one side, guys on the other. Rolling my coat into a pillow, I soon discovered how useless it was to relax on a wooden bench.

After one such concert, a fellow choir member had shown me to a waiting area where we'd retrieve our belongings for the trip home.

"You aren't just going to leave her there, are you?" shrieked an elderly woman.

"Oh, I'm coming right back," my companion told her.

"But she might fall off her chair!"

Embarrassed by this woman's outburst, I wanted to disappear into the over-stuffed furniture. What notions keep cropping into people's minds about me and chairs, anyway? In my quirky imagination, I fancied myself with a seatbelt descending from the heavens, strapping me in to hold me up.

•

As one might imagine, dating for me was another immense disappointment. Indeed, there was 'balloon-head,' the guy with an inflated ego who spoke on and on about his favourite subject, namely, himself. Sitting at a restaurant, I picked up my soda, unaware of the tilting straw in my glass. Phew! I was grateful for his incessant droning, as somehow he'd failed to notice how the straw had rudely poked up my nose.

And how could I forget 'sponge-brain,' the guy who attempted to drench every ounce of my spirit. Never did he introduce me to his family or friends, and clearly he didn't want to meet any of mine. His idea of 'wooing' me was a daytrip out of town, this way no one he knew would spot us together.

The one who crushed me the most, was the guy I met in my last year of high school. Although we got along well, I believe we were too immature for any sort of relationship. Wounding were his parting words:

"I don't think you'll ever get married." "Why!" I burst into tears.

"Because," he stammered, edging toward the door, "you're blind."

Until I had reached my thirties, this cutting scene reeled over and over in my mind. Could my desperate choices which ensued in balloon-head and sponge-brain be due to such an insensitive statement? I won't throw him under the bus too much, however — decades later, I would come upon a message from him on social media. He offered a sincere apology, saying, "I will understand if you can't forgive me." He meant it, and in time we developed a respectable friendship.

Admittedly, I might occasionally pray, "God, isn't there a special someone in this world who could share in my life?" Such pining, I realized, kept me from being the best version of myself. After all, I was content on my own — and why not? I liked to be independent and resourceful.

I had my faith, my music teaching career, and a supportive family. I felt I had arrived at a good place... Then, when it was least expected, God revealed he had other plans for me.

Chapter 17
IN GOOD TIMES, AND IN BAD

With the new teaching year ahead, I had most items checked off my to-do list: floors scrubbed, students registered, and braille books on the shelf organized by grade. Although, seeing that my typewriter was in the shop for repairs, the annual printed information I provided to parents would simply have to wait.

It was late afternoon when a voice on the other end of the phone identified himself, saying, "Hello. This is Michael, of Furlong Electronic Services." With barely time to acknowledge the man's greeting, he continued, "Question... how's your cat?"

My feline companions, Tigger and Jasper, were eight years old at the time. Seeing that I hadn't mentioned them before, I was curious. "How did you know that?"

"I thought so," he mused. "The fur in your typewriter was a dead give-away."

As we spoke, I learned that cleaning pet hair from equipment was all in a day's work for him. In good humour, he related instances of having fished out peculiar objects from machinery: coins, a man's watch, a cheese sandwich and even cooked spaghetti.

The following day, Michael and I were sitting at my kitchen table, the typewriter as its centrepiece. "Since it's on my way to the bank, I will deliver it to you," he had offered. In my recollection, he was nearly late for a weekly appointment as we lost track of time in yet another pleasant exchange.

How we started dating is somewhat hazy. I suppose after chatting for about ten hours — over two phone conversations and our eventual kitchen rendezvous — he was inclined to ask, "Would you like to go for a walk with me sometime?" And that's what we did... we walked, we talked, and we laughed.

It was August 28th, when arm in arm, we strolled across the Fredericton walking bridge. Overlooking the Wolastoq-Saint John River, Michael depicted a poetic scene of the little grassy islands, the ducks swimming past, while painting the evening stars as sparkling diamonds on the water. That did it! I was smitten!

Admittedly, there was a momentary hesitation when I discovered Michael was fourteen years older than me. Nonetheless, I had recognized that most people in my life tended to be of that generation, and, compared to guys closer to my age, I appreciated the maturity he showed.

Despite our age difference, Michael had an essence of youthfulness about him! Who else would barrel down Main Street through teaming rain while engaging in a contest of word banter?

"Did you ever see a house... fly?" he joked.

Envisioning a cartoon-like cottage jetting through the sky, I giggled. "No! Did you ever see a chimney... sweep?"

"Ha ha! You're good! Well then...have you ever seen a turtle... wax?"

I challenged, "Have you ever heard a tree... bark?"

As we leapt over random puddles, he swapped one more, "Have you seen a leg... iron?"

Stalling, I considered my comeback. "Have you heard an ear... drum?"

Yep, this was an absurd wash of wits, our repartee, and between a cloudburst and a car splash, the two of us were soaked from head to toe!

•

Without a doubt, life was a constant narrative with Michael Furlong. During one of our infamous walks, I sensed another story coming on as we passed by a cemetery in his neighbourhood of Devon.

"Oh, you'll like this!" he exclaimed, pointing to our right. "We kids use to wander here through the graveyard, and one day — a friends' leg went into a hole in the ground.

With the most ghastly look on his face, he screamed aloud, telling us that a hand had grabbed his foot! We didn't know whether or not to believe him, but none of us stuck around to find out!"

Further down a quiet street, we walked by the house which Michael's father built. "I really miss him," Michael's voice strayed, his father having passed away a year earlier. Slowing our pace, he gazed into the yard. "I remember when Dad used to make wooden airplanes for us. They were big enough for a three- to five-year-old to sit in,

and we'd pretend to be flying into the wild blue yonder."

Turning toward me, Michael's tone brightened. "I wish Dad had known you. He would've thought you were the cat's pyjamas!"

Although I did not have the opportunity to meet Michael's father, I believe they must have been very much alike. Each had mutual gifts in the areas of music and art, and both possessed abilities to build anything from scratch. Thereafter, I spent many hours keeping Michael company as he constructed his own radio-controlled aircraft. While he meticulously designed these large planes, each with a minimum six-foot wingspan, I'd knit, and listen, as he had endless tales to recount.

•

Unlike other guys, Michael was never someone who was ashamed of me. Quite the opposite, in fact. In no time, he
introduced me to his aunt Helen — a mother figure to him
— his cousin Sheila, who was more like a sister, and to his brother, Paul.

Another fond memory that impressed upon me was when he asked, "Will you come with me to the aircraft club's annual bonfire?"

"Um..." I answered in a shy manner. "I wouldn't want to be the only female there."

"Dear..." he said, holding both my hands in his, "wives and girlfriends will be there, too. Please, say yes. I'd be so honoured if you were there with me."

Could anything have been more charming than the rhythmic chirp of crickets and a crackling fire on this autumn's night? It started by meeting the most welcoming people, especially Michael's long-time friend, Fernand. Afterward, when everyone had eaten their fill of roasted hotdogs, we were entertained with Michael playing his beloved Martin guitar along with the lively accompaniment on Fernand's accordion. And throughout the entire evening, not once was I made to feel out of place with Michael so attentively by my side.

•

Having been welcomed by Michael's friends and family, he too would be acquainted with my own loved-ones, as well as with extended relatives in Grand Falls. Upon returning from one of our visits to northern NB, Michael and I stopped at a small diner on the old Trans-Canada Highway. During lunch, we noticed that the waitress was particularly disrespectful to those at an adjacent table.

When she came to serve us, Michael inquired, "Hi! What's on the dessert menu?"

In a single breath, she recited, "We have chocolate-peanutbutter-coconut-pie."

"Mmm! That sounds good," he replied.

"Which one?" she huffed.

"We'll have the one you just mentioned."

"No," the boorish waitress groaned. "It's chocolate-peanutbutter or coconut pie."

"Okay," Michael and I decided, "we'll take the chocolate-peanutbutter."

This time, our hostess made a rude spectacle of herself!

"No... we have chocolate! Comma! Peanut butter! Comma! And coconut pie, period!"

"I've never had peanut butter pie," I chimed in, attempting to ease the tension. "I'll take that, please."

"Oh!" she sniffed. "We're all out of that!"

With no surprise, Michael was obliged to report Miss Congeniality to the manager for her insolent and churlish behaviour. Even so, we would have our own story to tell, one which made us laugh for years to come. Who knows! Perhaps all this woman needed was to unwind with an extra large, comma, soothing slice of music! Period!

•

Ahh! Music! An intimacy, a spiritual oneness — both are inadequate to describe the connection Michael and I shared. What's more, it was humbling when soon we were invited to perform in churches, at senior's homes, and for numerous special events.

Beyond the concerts themselves, we were happiest when rehearsing together. It was an easy, fluid collaboration.

"You lead on the first verse, I'll take the second, and we'll sing harmony on the chorus."

Furthermore, nothing compares to those golden nuggets of time when you're with someone you love, doing something you love. As I recall, seldom would we go through a session without Michael cracking me up! Deliberately singing off key, he'd goof up the lyrics to songs, with "Brown Eyed Squirrel" or "PS, I Glove You."

•

Over the course of three decades, ownership in Furlong Electronic Services was an immense source of pride for Michael. All the same, as we had evolved into a plastic, throw-away society, the decline in his repair business weighed heavy upon him. Living off his savings, he struggled to come to terms with the inevitable. He would have to dissolve his company. Later, as he began to earn a steady paycheque in retail, Michael and I felt comfortable in taking the next step. We were getting married.

And to those naysayers who felt it was their place to whisper in Michael's ear, "Don't get too involved with that girl... You'll end up having to take care of her... You should just be friends," I now present my official, "*PFFFT!!*" What were they thinking? Surely, they must have known he was far too intelligent to give credence to such tongue-wagging!

•

Having a fresh start, we purchased a three-bedroom bungalow — the perfect house for us. With only Michael and I, one spare room was designated for his desk, computer, and musical instruments, while the other was ideal for my teaching studio. Using a bit of wedding money, Michael installed French doors leading to the living-room and kitchen area. A classic touch to our home, it also provided him with privacy when piano lessons were in session.

Although cliche, the thought of being a 'house-wife' was, for me, rewarding. While Michael was run off his feet at the store, there was a fulfillment in knowing I was the one who kept our home inviting, pristine and cozy. Still, with my piano teaching, this presented a task in time management. My goal was to make it look effortless: no dishes in the sink, no dust, no crumbs or spills; and when he walked through the door, the meals I prepared made a photo finish to the dinner table.

Despite my good intentions, life is a series of mishaps. When I flubbed up, Michael was ready to rub it in with a poke and a nudge.

"Did you forget something, Dear?" I was befuddled! Knowing the recipe by heart, how on earth had I neglected to mix the peanut butter into his favourite baked treat — peanut butter cookies?

Then came the shower curtain incident. I had decided to give our bathroom a thorough cleaning, walls, windows, floors, the whole thing. This accomplished, I retrieved the curtain from the washer and dryer cycle, and proceeded to hang it up...

Oh oh! Hmm, I wonder if he'll notice?

The next morning he observed, "The curtain seems awfully short. Did you buy a new one?"

"No," I answered. Reasoning that he'd be upset, I volunteered nothing else.

With an unusually hot summer in Fredericton, Michael hypothesized that the shrinkage may be due to the heat and humidity. After a few days of tussling with the trimmed down version of our shower curtain, he eventually brought one home, saying, "You did something to it, didn't you."

I had to fess up. We laughed, especially when he divulged, "Yeah, and you should have seen the looks I was getting from people at work when I told them our shower curtain had shrunk with this sweltering weather!" Sure! I can hear it now, the crumple of plastic curtains shrivelling throughout the city.

•

At some point, every couple will experience the vows of 'In Sickness and In Health.' Although Michael stood by me through my second knee replacement as well as another eye removal, the cure for what ails us are always in those thoughtful acts of kindness. Whenever arthritis took hold and I couldn't reach upward, he'd tenderly comb my hair and in his best Pepé Le Pew he'd say, "Bonjour Madame! Welcome to my salon. I am Michel, your coiffeur." And while the interminable common cold latched on to me for weeks at a time, the unexpected hum of laundry machines or a delightful aroma of an oven-roast chicken was just what the doctor ordered. Indeed, it's the pleasurable things I want to dwell upon — but sadly, I can't forget the times I would care for Michael in ways I couldn't have predicted.

•

Clearly, Michael loved his job, and well acquainted with all departments in the store, he was the one associate to whom the shoppers would make a direct beeline. Even for those kooky customers to which he'd privately tell me, "I don't suffer fools," his emphasis was on giving the best possible service to everyone.

Despite that, the relentless scourge of Michael's day was his boss, The Godfather. Sitting in his glass tower, he'd look down on the little people, his employees — waiting to pounce. Even when vacationing on his private yacht, he'd spy via technology through security cameras to catch his next victim. "You're spending too much time with the customer. You're not spending enough time with the customer. A customer is standing alone in aisle fifteen. Get moving! Why are you mixing paint when you should be in hardware stocking shelves..." And with each criticism, Michael became a shadow of his former self.

It was gradual, but I began to notice behavioural and physical changes in him. As he'd get snappish, I'd dither about asking, "Will you add flour to our grocery list, please?" or "Can you read the mail to me?"

All things simple became unfeasible for Michael. The accidental crash of dishes as they hit the floor was a common occurrence in our home. And like the plates and bowls he'd drop, his own confidence splintered into tiny pieces.

When after he had gone to work or perhaps in the middle of the night, I'd enter the kitchen, astounded to find a stove burner had been left on. "It's age," I thought, but more and more, I realized it was the undue stress he endured on the job.

What a despicable complaint! On the basis that Michael could no longer lift items over 100 pounds, his boss threatened to let him go. But with the holidays upon us, and given The Godfather relished the sound of his own voice, our hope was that his latest Scrooge-like tantrum would pass.

On January 4th, halfway through the workday, I heard the door open. Why was Michael home?

"What's going on?"

An expressionless, "I'm done," was all he had to say. In our living-room, I turned on the electric fireplace, giving an illusion of warmth to an otherwise bleak day. As I listened, I fully expected Michael to be livid. Instead, he spoke in the most dejected tone as though he were reliving the loss of his boyhood puppy. This wasn't like him. It made sense, however, as strip by strip, The Godfather had chiseled away at my husband's psyche — so much so, Michael had a worthless view of himself.

I was conflicted. One moment I was angry, thinking, "What a rotten, selfish thing to do — especially to a man whose retirement was merely one year away." On the other hand, perhaps it was a blessing. What if that toxic work environment were to cause Michael a heart attack before reaching 65?

•

Although Michael had every intention of seeking employment, each morning he'd experience a dry mouth, nausea and shakiness. In this agitated condition, there was no way he could go back to work.

And so, for six months, we coasted on my piano income. For six months, we buckled under stress. As if the walls were closing in, I faced yet another debilitating surge of arthritis while Michael succumbed to an emotional withdrawal: no family gatherings, no socializing with friends. The man I married, whom I suspect could have discussed life's deepest meaning with a fencepost, was now a recluse. And to that end, an overt distance carved between us, regrettably, became a wound from which we would not recover.

But with the dawn of summer, a glimmer of my Michael began to shine. Besides, is there a more carefree season in which to stroll together on moonlit evenings, to picnic in the park, or to visit a riding stable? Above all, I observed a renewed creativity in Michael as he sketched scenery for his model railroad village, and dabbled with music once again. And through our kitchen window, I distinctly heard a return of his infectious laughter while he chatted with the neighbours. At last, everything was right with the world, until it wasn't.

"Why is he being such a jackass," I murmured.

From the far end of the house, I could hear Michael grunting expletives while tugging at his clothes and whipping them into the air. The thing is, it wasn't just this morning, it was every morning. I approached and cautiously asked, "Can I help?"

"Yes, please," was a response I did not expect. I then realized my offer should have been made weeks ago, but I was afraid he'd be embarrassed.

It was early May, when assisting Michael with dressing became a part of our daily routine. But there was more to come, and if I didn't discover an incident myself, he was honest enough to tell me.

"You won't believe what I just did," he reported while walking toward me in the piano room. "I put instant coffee and sugar in my cup, then placed it in the microwave without water. Boy! What a mess!"

Although everyone slips up, I began to notice a disturbing pattern with Michael. There were more kitchen encores featuring burnt coffee as well as charred oatmeal. Then came the first episode with the running water. "He can't still be shaving?" I suddenly realized Michael wasn't in the bathroom at all, but that the faucet had been left on for the last twenty minutes.

Michael's explanation concerning his fall in the backyard, set off more alarm bells.

"What happened," I asked, as we went outside to search for his glasses.

"I don't know," he replied in bewilderment. "I was walking across the lawn. Then my legs went faster, and faster, and I couldn't stop them. The next thing I knew, I was laying on my face in the grass."

Perhaps the saddest moment was when he came to me saying, "I can't play my guitar."

"Maybe you're out of practice?"

"No," he explained, "My fingers won't stay in place.

I try, but I just can't form the chords."

During the next few months, Michael would undergo a series of medical tests and appointments. Oh, how he hated that! There were CT scans, MRI's, EEG's, an occupational therapist, an optometrist, a neurologist, and a geriatric specialist. For all of this, I was told it was either blood clots in his brain, mini strokes, moderate to advanced dementia, or something yet to be determined. If anything at all was established, it was in stoking a hellish anxiety in him.

•

On this October morning, everything started as usual. After breakfast, I sorted his clothes for the day as Michael headed toward the shower.

"I don't know where I am."

"What!" I exclaimed, rushing to his side. "You're at the bathroom entrance."

"I don't know what to do." "You're going to take a shower."

"But I don't know what order to do things in."

As terrifying as this was, I forced myself to remain calm. But as tears welled up, I turned away until the moment passed.

"Michael, you're already undressed." I took his hand to guide him, then rotating the tap, I adjusted the water temperature. "All you have to do is get in."

After this frightening ordeal, I applied for support through a government homecare program. Yes, I was overwhelmed, but Michael was never a burden to me. He was my husband, my partner. However, as my own health was tenuous, I knew this was the right decision for us.

By mid-November, help was on its way. "We'll spend more quality time together," I assured him. Alas, such promises are fleeting — on December 12th, Michael would be admitted to hospital.

•

It's snowing! It's way too quiet! Wandering about the house was our ten-year-old cat, Mattie. She'd behaved overly skittish since Michael left.

Call it instinct — on that day, his long-tailed protector circled round and round his feet, meowing as if to say, where do you think you're going?

"You be a good girl," he told her. "I'll be back."

•

At last, the phone rang —another winter storm had kept us apart. But as his speech has deteriorated, conversations went something like:

"When can I come home?" "I'm not sure."

Then, a lonesome pause. "I'll be there tomorrow, okay?"

This time we each echoed an "I love you," then I hung up and cried out in pitiful despair. "Oh! Michael! Please don't go!"

•

Sitting at his bedside, I reached under the covers to hold Michael's hand. I needed to touch him. How did we get here? Too long, yet too brief — the last seven months were but a jumbled blur.

As home assistance had been limited to four hours per day, ultimately, I remained as Michael's primary caregiver. But it was hard, really hard.

When Michael could no longer hold a fork, I was somewhat nervous about feeding him. What if I'm a bad aim? I might stick it in his ear! "Don't worry," he'd say. "You stab it, and I'll lean in to bite it."

His numerous tumbles to the floor were another mystery. Six times in two weeks, five of which occurred when I was alone with him. Arms around his chest, I'd hold him as though he were the most precious, fragile thing in my world. "God, don't let me drop him," I would pray.

"Try to grip with your feet," I pleaded, as his hands involuntarily dog paddled into mid-air. Using all my strength, I had miraculously lifted Michael into an upright position, again.

When Michael had lost his driver's license, right there to step in was his brother, Paul. "Is tomorrow, Friday?" he'd ask. After all, that was their day, and he knew Paul would be there bright and early. And thus, whether it was Christmas shopping, or chatting over a hot beverage at a local cafe, Michael cherished their time together.

•

As Paul and I had traded shifts, tonight was my turn. I'm certain Michael heard my voice. No, he couldn't speak, but as I related our own memories, a sudden twitch, a wordless utterance - confirmed his awareness.

"You remember, don't you." His hand gestured in recognition, as my computer played our wedding song.

"Me too. It was on August 28, just like our first date: so beautiful."

By no means is marriage a fairy tale, but how fortunate we were to have our 'Once Upon A Time' beginning to embrace within our hearts. Together, Michael and I, along with best man, Fernand, and maid-of-honour, my sweet sixteen-year-old niece, Erin, were escorted from the church in a horse-drawn carriage. Amongst the clip-clop of hooves, the sway of trees to a light breeze, the twitter of birds, and horns honking their congratulations, we couldn't have dreamed of a more perfect day.

"It's been a journey, hasn't it?" I stifled a sob and pressed my wet cheek to his chest. "You know how I hate goodbyes. I can't... Michael — I'll just say, till I see you... and when I do — you know it will be with my own two eyes."

•

At 10-AM, Paul arrived to stay with Michael while my sister, Joan, drove me home. As I fretted over household chores, Joan urged, "You haven't slept all night. Try to get some sleep. Don't worry... I'll do your dishes. Yes, I'll take the garbage bin out and clean the kitty litter, too. Just go to bed!"

As I lay down, I felt a lurch as Mattie bounded onto the bed. In the six weeks since Michael left, she'd been unusually quiet and standoffish. I was certain she missed his carryings-on during their lengthy conversations. "Hello," he'd say, which Mattie would mimic in a two-syllable meow and then purr her flirtatious excitement. He sure had a peculiar connection to that cat. But today, I think she sensed something was wrong. Clinging to me, Mattie simply wouldn't let go.

•

Around 4:00 PM, Joan picked me up from home again. As I had forgotten to bring snacks, she offered to purchase some at the hospital cafeteria for me.

In her absence, I leaned over and hugged my husband. "I'm here, Michael. I'm staying with you, all night." He exhaled deeply, acknowledging my presence. He was waiting for me, I'm sure of it! So much for the doctor's professional opinion. "In time," they said, "Michael won't know anyone." That couldn't have been further from the truth.

His breathing appeared more shallow than before, but being steady, I assumed it would continue throughout the night. Once more, I held Michael's hand, his cold fingertips imparting an uneasy chill. If only I could hear his voice. If only I knew what was going through his mind. If only...

Sometimes, there's a sense of isolation in blindness: the missed glances — the inability to make eye contact. I had often wondered, *what is Michael looking at?* The day I expressed this sentiment to Joan, her answer was exactly what I needed to hear. "He's looking straight at you... always!"

When she returned with refreshments, Joan asked, "Do you want me to stay a while?"

"You don't have to. I'll be fine; besides, I know you have work to do, and..."

"It's no bother. I'm staying," she resolved, and settled into a nearby chair.

Secretly, I appreciated her companionship. Now, sensitive to every breath Michael took, my sister and I sat, and talked, and listened — then... a stillness.

While caressing his arm, my voice choked, "It's okay, Michael."

Having alerted a nurse, my sister hurried back into the room. As a stethoscope was placed on Michael's heart, Joan and I waited to hear what we already knew. "I'm sorry," the nurse spoke softly. "He's gone."

Chapter 18
SONG OF LUMINESCENCE

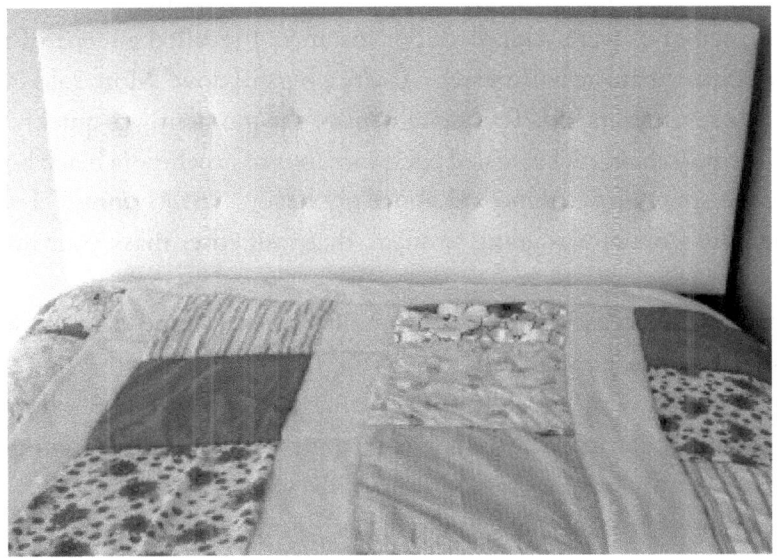

Retiring to my bedroom, I reached under my pillow and turned down the quilt. "It's not just any quilt, it's a braille quilt." That's what my mother called it, after she had made it especially for me. As though each textured patch were a separate chapter of my life, I peruse its surface to read the fine details, some with silky clarity, some with knotted questions.

Throughout my lifetime, the ongoing theme of my story has always centred around my physical well-being. After all, what I do from day to day, and sometimes from hour to hour, is contingent upon the level of pain and fatigue associated with rheumatoid arthritis. Although mental health is topical, I never thought it affected me; that is, until it was brought to my attention that perhaps what I've experienced is a moderate degree of Post Traumatic Stress Disorder.

Click! As though a lamp had been switched on, it shed a new perspective into my psyche. Things began to make sense: like my triggered response to a standard pandemic demand, "You must wear this medical mask." Of course, I am not condemning precautionary guidelines; I'm just saying — if I substitute by wearing multi-layered scarves to protect myself, perhaps a modicum of sensitivity from health professionals might be in order.

As I considered the attributes of PTSD — the nightmares, the flashbacks — other memories were rekindled. For instance, I recalled a scene of my first ever appointment at the hairdresser. "You're a big girl now," Mom told me when I was six or seven years old. The excitement of the moment was quickly doused in the shampoo chair. As I reclined backward, out of nowhere, a black hose with an attached spray nozzle appeared above my head, "No! Mummy!" I shrieked in panic. The woman was going to sneak that foul ether mask over my face, I just knew it!

Perceiving the cause of my fear, Mom lifted me from the chair, drawing my princess day to an undesirable close.

My behaviours can all be traced to that surgeon, the one who decades earlier physically constrained me and forced me to inhale that sickening gas. In some instances, my reactions are minimal: like when I change the TV channel away from shows featuring hospital settings, to experiencing an acute response to particular brands of toothpaste. Concerning the latter, I recall an incident when the menthol-infused goo in my mouth stunned me with that awful sensation of being put under, and instantly I felt as though I may pass out, right there on the bathroom floor.

Disconcerting, are the episodes which come about in public places, as evidenced while sitting in a dentist's waiting room. A few feet away, I overheard an assistant coax a child, saying, "Are you ready for some sleepy juice?" she asked with a syrupy sweet tone. "I promise, you won't feel a thing." Immediately, a wave of dizziness washed over me, along with a sudden urge to shout, "**LIAR!**"

Significant, are the multiple surgeries in which I refused to lay down as attendants rolled my stretcher into the operating room. I'd insist on remaining upright while the anesthesiologist inserted an IV into my hand, and the O.R. nurse held me until I fell asleep. This same scenario would repeat itself following that childhood ordeal, and well into my adult years.

When I was admitted for my second knee replacement, I learned that the O.R. nurse on duty was a former neighbour. I braced myself, fully anticipating my recurring drama would begin to unfold. Rather, I was comforted as she warmly spoke to me of her children who had grown up with my siblings. "Where is Thom now? How are Susan and Joan?" Distracted by our conversation, I somehow forgot I was lying down. There had been four decades of trauma but in that moment, our neighbourhood nurse demonstrated — no one was there to hurt me.

Since the onset of the pandemic, these childhood fears of a mask being forced over my face have resurfaced. In my head, I know it's irrational: yet, I can't shake the feeling of being a defenceless five-year-old on the operating table.

•

As I turn the page to my six years at the Halifax School For The Blind, I will be fair and acknowledge the camaraderie amongst students, the sincerity of houseparents and most of all, the invaluable instruction I received in braille literacy. Regardless, given my personal experience, I can't dismiss my true sentiments: the school building — a fire trap; the education — inferior; and prolonged segregation for kids like myself — unnecessary.

In order to validate or disprove my reservations, I contacted the Halifax Public Library. As a result, I received a number of articles and letters to the editor within the publication of "The 4th Estate" dated 1973.

While my mother read aloud to me, I could easily identify with the journalist's impressions of the school's interior. Guiding me once more down its corridors and into the classrooms and residence, were his less-than-flattering descriptions of dark and drab and grey. Hearing an outsider vividly portray the building and its accommodations as unsuitable for children, was eye opening. A signature of merit, however, were the thick banisters adorning the winding staircases, appropriately depicted as an architect's dream.

I admit, sliding down those old railings was a godsend on bad arthritis days. Nevertheless, I can attest to it not being an ideal atmosphere for me. While in this draughty, antiquated building, I constantly sought out places to keep warm, such as retreating to one of the piano practice rooms where the sun shone through the window, or to my semi-private dorm where my bed hugged against the radiator pipes.

The articles also drew attention to the HSB curriculum, pointing to numerous studies which were presented to the school's Board of Managers. Interestingly, the reports stipulated that the education was substandard and did not prepare students for the real world.

It reminded me of when, home on vacation, I'd hear what my younger siblings had been learning in school. Although a grade or two behind me, the books they read, the subjects they studied, appeared advanced in comparison to my own academics, leaving me with a feeling of inadequacy. One may argue, different provinces, different programs, but there were too many inconsistencies in my estimation.

Further to these reports, I can only surmise that the board of managers must have faced outside pressures. Suddenly, HSB had a new title: The Sir Frederick Fraser School, named after the founder and first superintendent from a century earlier. Along with this window dressing, our education also appeared to undergo an ever-so-slight change. Needless to say, the cynic in me ponders: was it all merely to promote a favourable image to the public? What planning was really invested into this curriculum remodel?

During this apparent evolution of the school for the blind, I recall when classes were put on hold in order for students to undergo SAT's and IQ tests. I was in grade seven at the time, and although I didn't realize the scope of this assessment, I eagerly accepted the challenge and worked my way through the transcribed braille pages.

A few weeks later, I was summoned to the vice principal's office. The man was practically hyperventilating as he revealed I had scored at a grade eleven level in math and reading comprehension. Boy! Why is he breathing like that? What is wrong with him? Oh, no! Is he going to bump me up four grades? Deep down, I always knew I had greater potential than the courses offered at this school, and now I had an affirmation.

As I think on that peculiar scene, it makes me more suspicious concerning the motives of superintendent, Mr. Olivier. Surely, my high IQ results would have reflected well on him — a feather in his cap as it were — an incentive towards his desperate efforts to keep me in Halifax.

While my mother continued to read from "The 4th Estate," she and I were astonished to learn that rumours of closing the school had circulated well before my arrival. I can understand as a child why I wouldn't be aware of this, but why was it not communicated to my parents? Then, as I had barely absorbed the information within the newspaper articles, came yet another blow.

•

Only in recent years have I reconnected on social media with former students of the Halifax School for the Blind. Honestly, I was struck by how many remembered me, particularly given my unceremonious exit. It was late evening when I was notified of posted audio files, one being the last formal closing I attended in 1978.

I was intrigued. I pictured my fourteen-year-old self sitting amongst my peers, and stubbornly tuning out the superintendent's voice. This time, however, I was prepared to listen.

Toward the end of the event, dozens of kid's names were called to receive prizes. Understandably, there were a few blips and pauses in the audio file — but was curious... where was I amongst the parade of recipients? In my memory, I don't recall ever going home without at least one award. By the same token, teachers of math, science, geography and history had noted on my final report card that I was top of the class, so it seems unlikely I came home empty handed. Besides, I distinctly remember Mr. Olivier's words of congratulations and... Never mind that — what I heard next, created a mini meltdown.

As Mr. Olivier stepped to the microphone for his final address, he announced: "To those students who will be coming back in the fall, we look forward to seeing you in September. For those who will not be returning, we will miss you." He then proceeded to introduce two or three students who would be attending public school in their respective hometowns. This was followed by an assurance that each one would be supported with assistance, along with a visit from a staff member of HSB to evaluate the student's progress.

How is it these statements did not register with me all those years ago? Better still, how would I process it now?

Provoking old resentments, once more I was shaken by the man who told me, "You'll never make it." And after a sleepless night I wrote in a message, "Can we talk," then sent it to a former student — the one named in Mr. Olivier's speech as continuing on to public school in New Brunswick.

•

On Sunday morning, the telephone chimed its long-distance ring. Her pleasant voice, her pragmatic approach to life made conversation easy and relatable. As we shared our differing circumstances, what stands out to me is that I was not the only one confounded by the actions of Mr. Olivier. "Yes," she confirmed, "they did provide me with braille books, as well as an itinerant teacher, I suppose around two hours per week."

"And was it you and your family who initiated the move into public school?"

"No," she clarified, "it was the administration in Halifax who encouraged it as part of their integration program."

Without disclosing her specific background, by her own admission she expressed that perhaps she wasn't the ideal candidate, whereas in her words, "You would have been the better choice, Cheryl."

As we recounted our individual experiences, I was even more baffled! Had the board of managers decided, "We'll assist protégé A, and deny protégé B?" Why the double standard? Was there a sincere goal on behalf of HSB to allow students to succeed in a sighted environment? Or, given that the school received $5000 per student from each of their home provinces, perhaps the rationale for the heads of administration was to maintain the status quo for their own benefit. What indeed was their agenda?

Certainly, I do not claim to understand what happened behind the scenes — nor what the inner workings were of the Halifax School for the Blind, as well as their collaboration with the Atlantic Provinces Special Education Authority and the various provincial governments. Whatever the case, they were responsible to provide the necessary tools in order for me to navigate through the public school system. For that, I give them a failing grade. And as for my fellow New Brunswicker and I, I would daresay that our individual achievements, for the most part, were due to our sheer determination.

While in Halifax, I was sustained by a flicker of hope — one day I will come home, live with my family, go to school, and be a normal kid. I couldn't wait! Granted, I was naive, and when life proved itself not as idyllic as I had imagined, that extra dose of tenacity would carry me through public school, and beyond.

I've conveyed how a system designed to facilitate my success, would be the very one to set obstacles in my way. Upon reflection, I can equally appreciate how the lack of resources must have impacted on my teachers, both in school and within my private music lessons. Nevertheless, I can see a tangible 'silver lining' in all of this, a perspective as revealed in a recent conversation with my Grade Nine homeroom teacher.

"You know," she confessed, "I believe you taught me more than I did you." She went on to explain how mindful she had become toward her students, observing their individual learning methods, whether it be through manual, visual or audio means. Truthfully, I expect she would have discovered these approaches over time but I appreciate her saying that I had an influence on her teaching career.

Another positive take-away comes from my longtime friend, Billy, who insists, "If it weren't for you, I would never have gone to public school." Initially, I thought of him as that shy, awkward blind guy who shared four classes with me in Grade Ten. What I did not realize was that Billy had lost his sight only two years earlier. When his mother had learned of my arrival on the scene, she was adamant that he not attend the school in Halifax. Instead, Billy would intermittently travel to Saint John, where, over a period of three months, he'd be immersed in mobility training, the basic rudiments of braille, and more beneficial for him the typing skills he had gained. Of course, I wouldn't be aware of his personal circumstances until our friendship developed years later. Had I known, I'd like to think that I would empathize, and offer him encouragement along the way.

In the meantime, I had a fierce resolve to demonstrate to the Halifax administration, and most of all to myself, that I wasn't there merely to survive, I was there to flourish. Toward that end, I needed more than to adapt academically, and music was the one complement to empower me with that necessary life balance. Ultimately, although we followed separate paths, I, along with Billy, would be the first totally blind students to graduate from Fredericton High School, perhaps even within the province.

•

In retrospect, it was instinctual when my mother said, "I worried about the consequences of sending Cheryl away... What if she became emotionally distant from her family?" Mom's concerns were justified — after all, how can any child not be effected when they are hundreds of miles from home, primarily raised by outsiders?

Innocently, I believed I would slip into the family unit right where we had left off, but over the six years, much had changed. While I was absorbed with a structured routine of homework and keeping pace with my sighted peers, it became apparent that my siblings had their own lives, their own friends; in essence, we had grown apart.

In adulthood, however, we found our way to each other. It was like getting acquainted all over again: to know what made them laugh, what made them proud, or to consider their own life's disappointments and respective pet peeves. Most of all, I could only hope that I would have their backs, the way they've always been there for me.

The epitome of their nurturing was openly evident during my campaign to promote Medicare coverage for prosthetic eyes. Not only did my immediate and extended family champion my cause, but I would receive immeasurable support from the general public along with friends and music colleagues.

The context of the matter was two-fold: that of healthcare, and of undue financial distress. Although I recognize where I live is one of privilege, I strongly maintain that no one should have to choose between pain and poverty.

It may seem strange, but I was relieved to have my eyes removed. The first one came after a long-standing battle with Glaucoma, resulting in constant headaches. As I recall, the second one was in conjunction with uveitis, where blood vessels would frequently burst, causing extreme burning, as though someone had puffed cigarette smoke directly into my eye. For that reason, I remained on morphine over a six-week period until I was admitted into the hospital.

Naturally, I was apprehensive over the idea of prosthetic eyes. But what were the alternatives: Live in pain? Exist with empty eye-sockets?

In the end, I was pleased with the outcome, but I hadn't realized it wasn't simply a 'once and done' scenario. Rather, as the prosthesis are composed of a plastic component which will gradually deteriorate, it makes it necessary to replace them approximately every five years. If neglected, chemicals will seep from the eye-socket into the bloodstream, spreading to the brain, and potentially being the cause of death.

At the time, the cost for prosthetic eyes was around $2000 each. Without medical insurance, this would create a financial burden on Michael and me. Again, my family, along with Michael's came to our rescue, substantially contributing to the overall expense.

"It can't go on like this," I thought, and after a decade of negative responses from successive health ministers, I was forced to take it to the media. Family and friends were also by my side: circulating a petition, making phone calls, writing letters to the editor and to government officials, as well as sitting at the legislature during a two-hour debate.

It was overwhelming! Regarding my family's persistence in advocating on my behalf, I have no words except to express it as articulated within excerpts from their own letters.

In his authoritative style, Michael writes:

> *Where a disability, in this case (blindness) comes to a person through no fault of their own, and is a working tax-paying resident of New Brunswick... elected officials are duty-bound to become educated on the issue before saying no to the cause.*

Through the sentimental words of my aunt Judy:

> *Cheryl Gillespie is my niece. I have witnessed the many struggles she has encountered all her life, and as the old saying goes, you never know what a situation is like until it hits home.*

Cheryl may be totally blind, but she is able to see things very clearly. Maybe it's time the NB government removed their blindfolds and reverse the decision on providing Medicare coverage for prosthetic eyes.

As for my youngest sister, Joan, she composed a lengthy letter which was both impactful and deeply heartfelt:

My sister was a pioneer, breaking down barriers for people with disabilities, opening the door for visually impaired children to remain at home with their families, and to enter public school instead of being institutionalized in a school for the blind, far from home. She worked twice as hard as any other student, and proved her only disability was society's inability to deal with challenge and change.

The government's reaction is for my sister to go on (welfare) in order to have medical coverage for this issue. Please tell me why this woman, a contributing member of our community, an author and piano teacher, should apply for monthly assistance? No, her income won't support prosthetic eye replacements every five years. But do we really want tax-payers to give her a monthly allowance when, other than this huge expense, manages quite well on her own?...This doesn't make financial sense.

As important as this is to me and to my family, it also demonstrates an obvious flaw in our social systems.... I believe that prosthetic eyes are not only medically necessary, but mentally necessary. Today's society is not kind to physical differences. I know. I take my sister shopping, and people go out of their way to STARE. So, if she were to lose this physical normalcy and have empty eye sockets, how do you think society will react? How will her young, school- aged students react?

My sister has fought multiple times for her life, her independence, her education and her health. She is the strongest human-being I know. She won't give up! All she asks, is for the dignity and respect she so deserves.

Finally, after a long day at the legislature, my mother wrote to a member of the opposition:

Dear Glen, I want to let you know what an excellent job you did today presenting the motion on Medicare coverage for prosthetic eyes. I could see that you did your homework and included everything that needed to be said. Cheryl has a very strong spirit and has accomplished a lot, but there are times when she needs the help of caring people like you.

And may I say, "Take that!" For this is just one example of my inclusive, proactive family of which I am blessed to be a part. And as a result of our collective lobbying, I was pleased to learn that a copay system was enacted, wherein patients with prosthetic eyes who have no medical insurance and who are not on social assistance, are currently eligible to have 80% of the cost covered by the provincial government.

•

The fabric of my life which intertwines with Michael's will never be forgotten. Since his passing in 2019, not a day goes by where I haven't thought of him; not one. Naturally, I can't pretend to idealize our marriage, as we were each independently minded and set in our ways. Yet, as patience and forgiveness prevailed, so too did Michael and I… and like a woven souvenir, the good memories are what I hold within my heart.

There are times, however, when I harbour some guilt, some bitterness. The guilt comes when I ponder, Did I do enough for him? His doctor quelled some of my insecurities in this area, saying, "I can't imagine how you were able to look after Michael as long as you did." The bitterness is toward Michael's boss, The Godfather. I agree: Michael likely had a genetic weakness concerning his illness, but I strongly believe that the mental abuse The Godfather inflicted on him, hastened his condition, robbing Michael and I of a few more precious years together. If I let it, these thoughts can tear me apart, which is why it is easier to focus on the positive.

It's the little things I miss, like when Michael would take time out of his day to meet each of my students at the door. Fluent in the gift of gab, he usually had observations like, "Wow, you got your hair cut!" Or, "Where did you buy that nice new jacket?" Oh, and it was a game for him to be on the lookout for those kids who arrived with flashy mismatched socks! I always cherished his visual icebreakers, as conversation openers often require more effort for me to make engaging.

As well, he definitely had a flair for describing the environment around us. Inclined to romanticize scenery, Michael would detail things like, "Oh, what a pretty garden!

Look! Its flowers are periwinkle and ivory, oh... and there's a little burst of fuchsia." Although it sounded dreamy, I recall asking for a comparison to blue, white or pink, as I had only learned primary colours when I was a child.

Yes, he was an inspired poet, but with a silly side, too. Michael would often make the birds have conversations, giving each one their own voice — the goofy grackle, the sassy robin or the busy woodpeckers. Even the trees would speak. "Hello Cheryl," he would say in a super deep tone, as though the nearby elm were greeting me!

Concerning our courting days, I remember how the tears would flow whenever Michael brought me home from a date. "Why are you crying?" he'd ask. "I'm not going anywhere. I'll be coming back." Poor Michael! Although my sobs were upsetting to him, I was unable to explain my emotions. In my grieving for him, I now recognize that deep abiding fear — if I allow myself to be vulnerable, I will eventually be left alone.

It's complicated: in one moment there's a huge void in my life, while in another, I am at peace with what Michael and I shared. He will live on, not only in my memory, but in his written words and songs.

IT'S MY HEART, TALKING TO YOU
Dedicated: To Cheryl, my loving wife.

(Verse Two)

In the stillness of the night time, if you hear somebody call,
It's my heart talking to you.

When you know there's no one else around, just you and I alone,
It's my heart talking to you.
When you reach out in the darkness for the love that's yours alone,
Don't worry 'cause I'm certain that you'll never feel forlorn.

The voice of one who loves you so is all you need to hear,
It's my heart, talking to you.

~Michael R. Furlong

•

Once more, my fingers scan the tactile braille quilt which my mother had made for me. A diverse sequence of velvety softness and bumpy dots are meticulously sewn together, as though to recite an intricate narrative. As I glance at a patch of sheer, almost see-through fibres, it somehow mirrors an old adage — we are all a little broken, that's how the light trickles in.

"There you are." Having claimed a spot on my bed, Mattie curls into a ball and purrs up a storm of her own. The soothing rumble beneath my hand, melts away all cares. "Aww, Mattie! It's getting late," I whisper, stroking her beautifully groomed fur. "Just one more goodnight lullaby, though," I speak to her in my sweetest cat-ese, then stroll back to the music room.

•

Beyond my window, another icy howl, and another snow-drift moulds a fortress around my house. I can understand Michael's aversion to the wind, but in some way the idea of a wintery white wall to provide insulation from the harsh, outside elements... appeals to me.

Gently, I reach for the hot cocoa which I had left on a nearby table. Warm to the touch, I drink every drop of its savoury milk chocolate. Setting down the empty cup, I then pull out my piano bench to rehearse another wistful song.

January: the month of fresh renewal for the future, and yet, tunes of old memories play in my head over and over again. On this winter's night, my fingers caress the piano keys of a soul-searching melody. Wishing it to last, I prolong the final chord until it fades to silence.

ACKNOWLEDGMENTS

I never dreamed I would experience an opportunity to reflect on our mutual backgrounds or to reminisce about my family who have ultimately shaped the course of my life. Toward that end — thank you to my parents, Shelia and Martin, for sharing your stories with me and for clarifying the events of my own past, specifically those when I was very young. A shoutout to my siblings, Thomas, Susan and Joan, who, after I had asked via e-mail to include your special memories, didn't hesitate to remind me of a few good ones. My gratitude also extends to Aunt Judy and Aunt Rebecca, each for shedding light on the heritage of the old homestead in Gillespie Settlement.

Writing an autobiography was the furthest thing from my mind; that is, until Garry Hanson, music teacher and longtime friend, raised the suggestion and the ideas began to flow. If it weren't for him, I'm certain this book would not exist. Thank you for the time spent on the phone, pressing me to analyze passages of my book and laughing with me over my novice blunders.

It was my good fortune to be recommended to Lee Thompson — an established author, editor, and book designer. Upon first impressions, I considered how readily he had accommodated my needs as a non-sighted writer. There are many who would not have recognized the visual practices of coloured highlights, or text in the margins as being ineffective when communicating with blind individuals. And yet, intuitively, Lee adapted his correspondence wherein my talking computer, Moses, could easily read to me his careful advice and attention to detail. Lee, thank you for coaching me on how to be a better writer, and making *I Feel Your Stare* evolve into what it has become today.

It would be difficult to name everyone, but I'd like to close by thanking my Goodine and Gillespie relatives, along with my numerous friends and colleagues who have expressed an interest throughout the process of my writing journey. To all of you who have offered words of encouragement, your support has meant more to me than you will ever know.

~Cheryl

ABOUT THE AUTHOR

In her home province of New Brunswick, Canada, Cheryl Gillespie, along with her cat Mattie, will often be found basking on the backyard deck beneath the warm sunshine, the very spot where many of the chapters for *I Feel Your Stare* were written.

A childhood diagnosis of Juvenile Rheumatoid Arthritis, with associated blindness, coupled with physical and societal barriers, has proven only to strengthen her resolve. Following graduation from Fredericton High School, Cheryl advanced in her private studies through the Royal Conservatory of Music, attaining First Class Honours in piano, theory and history. Today, well established in her teaching career, she takes pride in the education of her students, highlighted by a two-time provincial medal winner through Mount Allison's Local Centre Examinations Department of Music. Through her active role within the Fredericton Music Teachers' Association. Cheryl has built invaluable, longstanding friendships with her colleagues.

In 1993, Cheryl was the recipient of the Stanley B. Cassidy Memorial Award, presented by the Fredericton Music Society, recognizing her dedication to excellence and personal achievements.

Cheryl's first work for adults, *I Feel Your Stare* was preceded by her children's book, *Tigger and Jasper's New Home*.

www.ingramcontent.com/pod-product-compliance
Lightning Source LLC
Chambersburg PA
CBHW060059190426
43202CB00030B/2849